BILL JOHNSON

IN THE
WATER

60 Days *in the* Overflowing Presence *of the*
Holy Spirit

WHITAKER
HOUSE

Scripture quotations marked (NKJV) are taken from the *New King James Version*, © 1979, 1980, 1982 by Thomas Nelson, Inc. Used by permission. All rights reserved. Scripture quotations marked (NASB) are taken from the *New American Standard Bible®*, NASB®, © 1960, 1962, 1963, 1968, 1971, 1972, 1973, 1975, 1977, 1995 by The Lockman Foundation. Used by permission. (www. Lockman.org). Scripture quotations marked (NIV) are taken from the *Holy Bible, New International Version®*, NIV®, © 1973, 1978, 1984, 2011 by Biblica, Inc.® Used by permission. All rights reserved worldwide. The "NIV" and "New International Version" are trademarks registered in the United States Patent and Trademark Office by Biblica, Inc.® Scripture quotations marked (AMPC) are taken from *The Amplified® Bible, Classic Edition*, © 1954, 1958, 1962, 1964, 1965, 1987 by The Lockman Foundation. Used by permission (www.Lockman.org). All rights reserved. Scripture quotations marked (TPT) are taken from The *Passion Translation*,® © 2017, 2018, 2020 by Passion & Fire Ministries, Inc. Used by permission. All rights reserved. (ThePassionTranslation.com). Scripture quotations marked (KJV) are taken from the King James Version of the Holy Bible.

Boldface type in the Scripture quotations indicates the author's emphasis.

The forms LORD and GOD (in small caps) in Bible quotations represent the Hebrew name for God *Yahweh* (Jehovah), while *Lord* and *God* normally represent the name *Adonai*, in accordance with the Bible version used.

IN THE WATER:
60 Days in the Overflowing Presence of the Holy Spirit

Bill Johnson
https://bjm.org/

ISBN: 979-8-88769-306-4 | eBook ISBN: 979-8-88769-307-1
Printed in the United States of America
© 2024 by Bill Johnson

Whitaker House | 1030 Hunt Valley Circle | New Kensington, PA 15068
www.whitakerhouse.com

Library of Congress Control Number: 2024943527

1 2 3 4 5 6 7 8 9 10 11 ᴜᴜ 31 30 29 28 27 26 25 24

CONTENTS

INTRODUCTION:
LIVING IN THE OVERFLOWING PRESENCE

Through this devotional, I invite you to immerse yourself in a deeply personal relationship with the Holy Spirit and allow Him to teach you His wonderful ways and purposes. When we speak of "learning" something, we often think of outlines, steps, points, or principles. And while we may use such resources, our hearts are where our primary learning takes place. *In the Water: 60 Days in the Overflowing Presence of the Holy Spirit* is designed for the learning of the heart. As I write in this book, *insight is meant to lead to encounter.* In other words, whatever knowledge about God and His Spirit we receive should lead to a deeper relationship with Him. God wants to fill us with His presence in such a way that everything about us is saturated with the God of wonders, the Holy Spirit who dwells in us and among us.

As you progress through this devotional, you will realize that nothing in life is mundane once God touches it by His Spirit. You have the opportunity to see and experience how the natural elements of life become supernaturally empowered through God's presence.

The Holy Spirit is a living, healing, powerful river, and He desires to fill you to overflowing. The psalmist said, *"My heart and my flesh cry out for the living God"* (Psalm 84:2 NKJV). Notice what is expressed in this verse: *"My heart **and** my flesh."* It is possible for the human body (flesh) to reawaken the appetite for the Holy Spirit that we were originally created with. It doesn't happen simply because we try to awaken it. That is beyond human talent or determination. It occurs in a realm that we can only surrender to and yield our way into.

We were already designed with this potential in mind. There's something transformational about being in the presence—the overwhelming presence—of the Spirit of God. It's not one-stop shopping or five minutes of singing "Amazing Grace" that brings change. Transformation involves a continuous yielding to the glory of the almighty One. It comes in measures and dimensions that must be stewarded for increase. Our going *"from glory to glory"* (2 Corinthians 3:18 NKJV, NASB) was God's idea and plan, and we experience continual increase through our faithfulness to remain in the Presence.

Let us move into the life-giving current of the Holy Spirit and begin living daily *In the Water.*

PART ONE:

IMMERSED

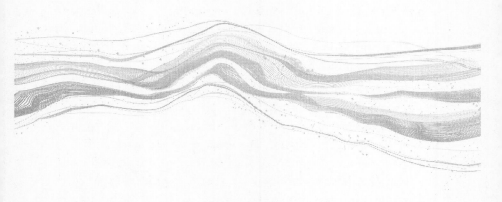

DAY 1

AN INVITATION TO KNOW HIM

"But the Helper, the Holy Spirit, whom the Father will send in My name, He will teach you all things, and bring to your remembrance all things that I said to you."
—John 14:26 (NKJV)

In many ways, the Holy Spirit is a mystery to us. We understand more about Jesus, who lived on earth for thirty-three and a half years, than we do the Holy Spirit, who has been with the church on earth for almost two thousand years.

On a surface level, it is much easier for us to know more about Jesus than we know about the Holy Spirit because it is simpler to relate to someone who is in the flesh—human, like we are. Most of us don't yet recognize that, at our essence, we are spiritual beings who have a soul and a body. Because of this, we usually think and live from the natural world toward possible spiritual experiences and realities rather than from the spiritual world. In the Scriptures, we are given a clear description of Jesus, who revealed the heavenly Father. Whether by reading about Jesus's conversations, His working of miracles, or His profound teachings, finding a practical connection to Jesus is easier than relating to the Spirit of God, whom we can't see or even properly imagine, even with various descriptions of His manifestations in the Bible.

When God led the Israelites in the wilderness, His face was in the cloud that traveled with them. (See Exodus 13:21.) In the original languages in both the Old and New Testaments, "presence" is literally "face." It fits the Lord's command to us to "seek His face," to which the psalmist replied, *Your face, LORD, I will seek* (Psalm 27:8 NKJV). The face of God is our ultimate quest.

However, God wouldn't let the Israelites see any form of Himself because He knew them to be an idolatrous people who would create an image from what they saw. We are presented with a similar challenge of "seeing" God today. The Holy Spirit remains the face of God on the earth, yet He does not have a form we can see.

Although the Holy Spirit is impossible to measure or quantify, this does not mean He is impossible to encounter. Many people envision the Holy Spirit as merely a force, an energy, or a "cosmic fog." But He is a divine person. As such, He understands you more fully than any human being does, and He can communicate with you in a way no other person could possibly do. In fact, having a personality, the Holy Spirit is relational by nature. He always rejoices in having a heartfelt connection with those made in God's image.

The relational nature of the ever-present Holy Spirit and His loving heart toward us show us that *we must come to know Him.* Personally. The revelation of this nature is, in itself, an invitation to know Him. Understanding and accepting this invitation is essential for everyone because, in knowing Him, our purpose for being unfolds.

⌒

Overflow: The Holy Spirit understands you more fully than any human being does, and He can communicate with you in a way no other person could possibly do.

Reading: John 14:19–26

Reflection: Have you accepted the Holy Spirit's invitation to know Him personally?

_____

_____

_____

_____

_____

_____

_____

_____

_____

_____

_____

_____

_____

_____

_____

_____

_____

_____

_____

DAY 2

RIVERS OF LIVING WATER

"If anyone thirsts, let him come to Me and drink."
—John 7:37 (NKJV)

The Holy Spirit and His works are put on display, like a fine art exhibit, throughout the New Testament. Everywhere we see Jesus, we see the Holy Spirit working, always to the glory of the Father. In John 7, Jesus describes the Holy Spirit as a river:

> *On the last day, that great day of the feast, Jesus stood and cried out, saying, "If anyone thirsts, let him come to Me and drink. He who believes in Me, as the Scripture has said,* **out of his heart will flow rivers of living water."** *But* **this He spoke concerning the Spirit,** *whom those believing in Him would receive; for the Holy Spirit was not yet given, because Jesus was not yet glorified.* (John 7:37–39 NKJV)

The Holy Spirit is likened to a river in us. Rivers *flow*, affecting everything they touch. They are continuous and ongoing, bringing life wherever they go.

Droughts are devastating natural events that are in stark contrast to flowing water. We have had several years of drought where I live in Northern California. Yet despite this severe lack of rain, the trees along the Sacramento River never seem to know there is a drought;

they are clueless. They are planted next to a continuously flowing river that is beautiful and exciting. I have spent many hours on this river, and it is exhilarating. The trees there thrive—and it is the same for all who abide in the presence of God: He is a never-ending river of life.

> *He shall be like a tree planted by the rivers of water, that brings forth its fruit in its season, whose leaf also shall not wither, and* **whatever he does shall prosper.** (Psalm 1:3 NKJV)

The river of the Holy Spirit that flows *from* us will first have a transformational impact *on* us. While the challenges of life are always with us, the fact that we're planted by a river has put us in a place of continual influence by the Spirit. I love the outcome: "*Whatever he does shall prosper.*"

The indwelling Holy Spirit is a river that is to flow from us, bringing life to everything He touches. Perhaps this is what the woman with the issue of blood discovered when she reached out and touched Jesus as He was passing by. (See Luke 8:43–48.) Life flowed from Him. Presence flowed from Him. Healing flowed from Him.

Is it possible to expect that the same life would flow from His disciples? I think so. To expect less is to diminish the work of the cross that qualifies us for all that Jesus taught, modeled, and commanded. Jesus's statement, "*He who believes in Me, the works that I do he will do also; and greater works than these he will do, because I go to My Father*" (John 14:12 NKJV), comes into play here. We were designed for greater. We were created for greater. We were redeemed for greater.

~

Overflow: The river of the Holy Spirit that flows *from* us will first have a transformational impact *on* us.

Reading: Psalm 1

Reflection: How can you plant your life more deeply by the River of Living Water so that you can draw from its waters at all times?

_____

_____

_____

_____

_____

_____

_____

_____

_____

_____

_____

_____

_____

_____

_____

_____

_____

_____

_____

_____

DAY 3

THE SPIRIT GIVES LIFE

"It is the Spirit who gives life; the flesh profits nothing. The words that I speak to you are spirit, and they are life."
—John 6:63 (NKJV)

There was something life-changing in the voice of the One who called the early disciples to Himself. Here is an account from the book of Matthew about the calling of several of them:

> Now as Jesus was walking by the Sea of Galilee, He saw two brothers, Simon who was called Peter, and Andrew his brother, casting a net into the sea; for they were fishermen. And He said to them, "Follow Me, and I will make you fishers of men." Immediately they left their nets and followed Him. Going on from there He saw two other brothers, James the son of Zebedee, and John his brother, in the boat with Zebedee their father, mending their nets; and He called them. Immediately they left the boat and their father, and followed Him.
>
> (Matthew 4:18–22 NASB)

What is it that would pull four men from their occupations, which had been passed down from their fathers, into an unknown journey with a relative stranger? Following always requires leaving something behind. These men left their fathers, boats, and nets. I can't imagine that their decision went over well with their families, as the occupation of fishing required the full attention of all on board. No doubt, this fishing business was to be their inheritance. But they left it all and followed Jesus—with actions that shouted *yes* to their new mission in life.

It's also important to note that Jesus made no promises of success to get them to follow. When He gave the invitation, what was already in their hearts, what was previously unrecognized by everyone else, came to the surface in that divine moment: it was their wholehearted commitment to God.

The disciples followed Jesus, indeed. But to where? Wherever He went. Of all the journeys ever taken, this one, more than any other, was not about the destination. It was entirely about the journey itself. *They were with Jesus.*

The disciples recognized that Jesus changed the atmosphere everywhere He was present. No exceptions. Whether He was alone with the Twelve, spending time with individual disciples one-on-one, or standing before thousands, He brought the tangible presence of heaven to earth. He lived the manifestation of the kind of prayer He taught them to pray: *"On earth as it is in heaven"* (Matthew 6:10, various translations). And the presence of God—the Holy Spirit—was released whenever He spoke. The John 6:63 principle was at work: *"It is the Spirit who gives life; the flesh profits nothing. The words that I speak to you are spirit, and they are life"* (NKJV). The disciples watched Jesus model what He told them so clearly: "I only say what I hear My Father say; I only do what I see My Father do." (See, for example, John 5:19.) Whether they understood this concept or not, they felt it. And it marked them. Jesus's words became *"spirit"* and *"life."* His words released His presence. And that presence was a life-giving force that changed everything.

⌒

Overflow: The presence of God—the Holy Spirit—was released whenever Jesus spoke.

Reading: 1 Corinthians 15:45

Reflection: What words of *"spirit"* and *"life"* has Jesus spoken to you? How have these words changed you?

_____

_____

_____

_____

_____

_____

_____

_____

_____

_____

_____

_____

_____

_____

_____

_____

_____

DAY 4

EMPOWERED BY THE HOLY SPIRIT

*"Then Jesus returned in the power of the Spirit to Galilee, and
news of Him went out through all the surrounding region."*
—Luke 4:14 (NKJV)

Imagine being in crowds where everyone is pushing and shoving
to get close to Jesus, and yet you have the privilege of being within
arm's reach of Him at almost any time of the day or night because
He *chose* you. The disciples' sense of personal significance could never
have been higher than at that time. But neither do I think they would
have had the notion that they somehow had earned or deserved this
opportunity. It was so far above what any person who had ever lived
had experienced. That included their heroes, like Moses, David, and
Isaiah. There was little chance of self-aggrandizement because they
lived with a consciousness of the grace they had been given.

And then imagine beholding miracles that had never been seen
before—by anyone! The disciples had a front-row seat to the miraculous, heaven's invasion of earth, which operates outside of human logic
and reason. It must have been exceedingly wonderful, mind-boggling,
and—above all—*inviting*. And as if that weren't enough, the Master
then equipped them to do the same. Yes, to do the same astounding
miracles and deliverances they saw come from Him. They must have
been overwhelmed by the fact that their personal story in ministry
had already involved seeing the hand of God manifest in miraculous ways. But the acceleration they were now experiencing, which

included their own unqualified participation in the working of miracles, must have stretched their imaginations to the breaking point.

The apostles' normal life activities of fishing, dealing with public officials, and following a religious routine had all lost their luster. Something had been awakened in them that would never be satisfied by anything other than the Jesus way of life. The Spirit of God resting upon the Son of Man had forever transformed everything. Only Judas Iscariot, who never dealt with the issue he had brought with him into his relationship with Jesus (the love of money), couldn't see beyond the immediate benefit or cost of following the One.

Jesus was a movement in Himself. He hosted the Spirit of God in a way that no king, prophet, or priest had done before Him. The crowds were overwhelmed by His miraculous works, displayed as the ultimate revelation of the Father's heart for His creation. And they were stunned by Jesus's words, confessing they had never heard anything like them: *"For He taught them as one having authority"* (Matthew 7:29 NKJV). It became obvious to them that all the other voices spoke without authority. Those voices were just noise. Ideas. Ineffectual commands. There was no life-changing power in them. The contrast between what the people were now hearing and what they had heard for their entire lives was stunning.

The disciples learned by experience what Jesus was teaching them about His life focus: pleasing the Father. Everything He did and said came from the Father, empowered by the Holy Spirit.

Overflow: Jesus hosted the Spirit of God in a way that no king, prophet, or priest had done before Him.

Reading: Luke 4:14–36

Reflection: What can we learn from Jesus's focus of pleasing the heavenly Father?

_____

_____

_____

_____

_____

_____

_____

_____

_____

_____

_____

_____

_____

_____

_____

_____

_____

_____

DAY 5

THE SPIRIT REMAINED ON JESUS

"He upon whom you see the Spirit descending and remaining upon Him, this is the One who baptizes in the Holy Spirit."
—John 1:33 (NASB)

The Holy Spirit dwells in every believer, but He doesn't always *rest upon* every believer at all times. He rests upon those who are fully yielded to Him, as Jesus was. Giving the Holy Spirit place, giving Him the opportunity to fully express Himself, is what Jesus modeled for us. He taught us how to honor and host this glorious Holy Spirit.

The Holy Spirit lives *in* me for my sake. But He comes *upon* me for the sake of others, to release the Spirit to them. The same Spirit that anoints me for ministry, comforts and directs me for life. When He rests upon me, it is always to bring transformation to my surroundings. Jesus exemplified this truth perfectly. It started at His water baptism, and this aspect of Jesus's story should impact the life of every believer. It is described in this way in John 1:33 (NASB): *"He upon whom you see the Spirit descending and **remaining** upon Him, this is the One who baptizes in the Holy Spirit."* The Holy Spirit descended upon Jesus and remained. Although Jesus came to earth with authority, as He was commissioned by the Father, He still needed spiritual power to do all the Father had intended Him to accomplish. His water baptism was the moment when He was clothed with the power of the Holy Spirit. This was both His water baptism and His Spirit baptism. Only after this experience do we see Jesus walking in power for ministry. This may be seen clearly in Luke 3:21–22; 4:1–30.

What stands out to me is the emphasis on the Holy Spirit *"remaining"* on Jesus. The implication is that the Spirit of God could have been there one moment and gone the next—in other words, He might not have been a constant or an ever-increasing reality there. But Jesus hosted Him brilliantly, never violating the Spirit of God in any way. He became the perfect resting place for the Holy Spirit.

When I tell this story of Jesus's baptism to groups, I often ask people, "If I had a dove, in the natural, resting upon my shoulder, how would I walk around this room if I wanted it to stay?" "Carefully" is the most frequent answer, and it's accurate. But I'd rather describe it in this way when thinking of my relationship with the Holy Spirit: every step I'd take would be with the dove in mind. Every movement would be to protect and honor what I value most—*Him*.

⌣

Overflow: The Holy Spirit lives *in* me for my sake. But He comes *upon* me for the sake of others, to release the Spirit to them.

Reading: Luke 3:21–22; 4:1–13

Reflection: How are you honoring and hosting the Holy Spirit in your life?

_____

_____

_____

_____

_____

_____

_____

_____

_____

_____

_____

_____

_____

_____

_____

_____

_____

DAY 6

WATCHING THE HOLY SPIRIT AT WORK

"He went about doing good and healing all who were oppressed by the devil, for God was with Him."
—Acts 10:38 (NASB)

The lifestyle of Jesus presents us with one continuous story of perfect partnership between a man and the Holy Spirit. Now, lest you think, as some have mistakenly reported, that I don't believe Jesus to be the Son of God, or God in human form, let me affirm this: He is the eternal Son of God! If He is not God, we have no salvation or promise of eternity! But He identified Himself as the Son of Man to illustrate what could be possible for one person who is completely surrendered to the Holy Spirit. It was the Holy Spirit who enabled the humanity of Jesus to perfectly fulfill the will of the Father on earth. The Holy Spirit is the One who enables us, too, to succeed in all the Father has assigned us to be and do.

One of my favorite Bible verses is Acts 10:38 (NASB):

*You know of Jesus of Nazareth, how God anointed Him with the Holy Spirit and with power, and how He went about doing good and healing all who were oppressed by the devil, **for God was with Him.***

When this verse states that *"God was with Him,"* it is not implying that Jesus wasn't God. It is emphasizing the fact that God was
with Him in His humanity. This is what made it possible for the Son
of Man to do all the Godlike things He did. In fact, at the very beginning of His ministry, Jesus announced that God was with Him:

> *The Spirit of the* LORD *is upon Me, because He anointed Me to*
> *preach the gospel to the poor. He has sent Me to proclaim release*
> *to the captives, and recovery of sight to the blind, to set free those*
> *who are oppressed, to proclaim the favorable year of the* LORD.
>
> (Luke 4:18–19 NASB)

Once more, we see that it was the Holy Spirit upon Jesus that
enabled Him to do all that He did. It was because God was with
Him that it could be said that He healed *"all who were oppressed by
the devil"* (Acts 10:38). It's not that every person alive was healed or
delivered. It was that everyone who came to Him, and everyone the
Father directed Him to, received their miracle. No exceptions.

When we read about the three and a half years of Jesus's ministry,
we're not always conscious of the fact that we are watching the Holy
Spirit at work. But the beautiful thing is that, in those moments, we
witness a revelation of the perfect union and manifestation of the
Trinity: Father, Son, and Holy Spirit. Through the works and words
of Jesus, we see the heart of the Father, manifested through the life,
nature, and work of the Holy Spirit.

It is our greatest honor to host this One who longs to reveal and
glorify Jesus. And it is Jesus who always points to the Father. Such
mystery, beauty, and wonder!

Overflow: It was the Holy Spirit who enabled the humanity of Jesus
to perfectly fulfill the will of the Father on earth.

Reading: Acts 10:34–48

Reflection: In what ways have you watched the Holy Spirit at work in your life?

_____

_____

_____

_____

_____

_____

_____

_____

_____

_____

_____

_____

_____

_____

_____

_____

_____

_____

DAY 7

TO OUR BENEFIT THAT JESUS LEFT EARTH?

"It is to your advantage that I go away."
—John 16:5–7 (NASB)

Toward the end of His three and a half years with His twelve disciples, Jesus brought them a revelation that was almost as far outside the disciples' ability to grasp as were the miracles He performed:

> *But now I am going to Him who sent Me; and none of you asks Me, 'Where are You going?' But because I have said these things to you, grief has filled your heart. But I tell you the truth, it is to your advantage that I go away; for if I do not go away, the Helper will not come to you; but if I go, I will send Him to you.*
> (John 16:5–7 NASB)

Hearing that Jesus was leaving them must have been a shock. But the real challenge came when He said His leaving was *to their advantage*. He easily could have said it was important for Him to leave because He was going to atone for their sins so that they could be born again, and that was the advantage. He might have said He was going to rise from the dead and intercede for them before the Father, and this was to their profit. Both statements would have been absolutely true. But, this time, His focus was on the one gift that was so far beyond all the rest of life itself that nothing else deserved immediate attention. He told them that after He left, He would send them *"the Helper,"* the Holy Spirit.

To their *"advantage"*? That would be hard to believe if you were one of the disciples, currently within arm's reach of the most amazing Person, God Himself in the flesh, walking the earth. Not since Adam and Eve walked with God in Eden in the cool of the evening had anyone been given the chance at such a practical yet profoundly impactful relationship with God in person. (See Genesis 3:8.) How was it possible that Jesus's sending the Holy Spirit, the Helper, was to their advantage over this Edenic experience?

And yet it was. And if it still seems to us like it would be better to have Jesus on earth in the flesh, then we're missing the main point of what He has made available to us: the One whom we can't live without if we are to live the life that Jesus calls us to. Having the Spirit's abiding, indwelling presence is greater than having Jesus with us in the flesh, within arm's reach.

One of the meanings of the Greek word translated as *"advantage"* in John 16:7 is "to be profitable."[1] A profit is basically an increase from an investment. Jesus promised the apostles they were about to receive an increase of their investment of time with Him. It would be an increase of all they had seen, heard, and experienced for the past three-plus years. There has never been a profit or an upgrade equal in significance.

⌒

Overflow: Having the Spirit's abiding, indwelling presence is greater than having Jesus with us in the flesh, within arm's reach.

Reading: John 16:5–15

---

1. *Strong's Exhaustive Concordance of the Bible*, G4851, Blue Letter Bible Lexicon, https://www.blueletterbible.org/lexicon/g4851/kjv/tr/0-1/.

Reflection: Jesus's departure from earth and the Spirit's coming to us as *"another Helper"* (John 14:16) is to our complete advantage, just as it was for the apostles. What advantages to this exchange can you list?

_____

_____

_____

_____

_____

_____

_____

_____

_____

_____

_____

_____

_____

_____

_____

_____

_____

_____

DAY 8

"ANOTHER, BUT EXACTLY THE SAME"

"I will ask the Father, and He will give you another Helper,
that He may be with you forever."
—John 14:16 (NASB)

I'm a bit embarrassed to say that, several times in recent months (the most challenging season of my life), I found myself saying or thinking, "God, I don't know what I'm doing. I wish You were here, sitting in that chair across the table from me, so You could tell me what to think and do." This cry for Him was both notable and legitimate. It was as sincere as you can imagine. My awareness of my personal need was also legitimate. But in a strange way, that cry of my heart was very similar to the cries of the Israelites in the wilderness, longing to go back to Egypt. As glorious as it would be to have Jesus sitting with me at my table, the reality is, He *is*. The indwelling Presence is sitting at every table where I sit. My awareness of Him, my conscious attention to all that He has said and is saying, is the very thing that positions me to offer my breath, my life, for eternal purposes. Only in offering myself in that context will I be able to leave a mark on the course of history that truly brings Jesus glory.

In the final week of Jesus's earthly life, He had many closing remarks for His disciples. He explained to them about the Spirit—the Helper, the legal Advocate, the Comforter, the One called alongside to assist them—who was coming to be with them:

*I will ask the Father, and He will give you another Helper, that He may be with you forever; that is the Spirit of truth, whom the world cannot receive, because it does not see Him or know Him, **but you know Him** because He abides with you and will be in you.* (John 14:16–17 NASB)

The Greek word translated *"another"* in this verse indicates "another, but exactly the same." Jesus was letting His disciples know that this Helper, the Holy Spirit, who had been resting upon Him during His entire three and a half years of ministry, was exactly the same as He was, with no variation. The Holy Spirit ensures such exactness of ministry, with no loss whatsoever. Everything the disciples had with Jesus, and everything they loved about Him, they would have with and love about the Holy Spirit. He added that they *already knew Him.* Since they knew Jesus, and the Spirit of God was exactly the same as He was, they knew the Spirit of God as well.

Jesus told them, *"He abides with you and will be in you."* In "phase two" of their life with Jesus (after His return to heaven), the Holy Spirit—the atmosphere of heaven they'd been living in because of Jesus, who is the Spirit's ultimate resting place—would take up residence in them. He would not just be *with* them. He would now be the indwelling presence of God.

⌒

Overflow: Everything the disciples had with Jesus, and everything they loved about Him, they would have with and love about the Holy Spirit.

Reading: John 14:1–20

Reflection: Do you sometimes wish that Jesus were sitting across the table from you in the flesh, especially when you are experiencing difficulty? How does it encourage you to know that the Holy Spirit, who lives within you, is exactly the same as Jesus?

DAY 9

"PEACE TO YOU!"

"He breathed on them, and said to them,
"Receive the Holy Spirit."
—John 20:22 (NKJV)

Immediately after Jesus was crucified, fear gripped the remaining eleven disciples so much that they went into hiding. Not even the fact that Peter and John had seen the empty tomb helped to calm the nerves of the terrified group following this traumatic experience. They had seen the brutal death of their Master. Their identity was widely known to people, so much so that a servant girl could tell that Peter was a follower of Jesus. (See, for example, Mark 14:66–72.) They were certain they would be killed next, as that is the way the Roman government worked.

The disciples hid in a room in an unnamed location. Upper or lower level, no one knows. All we know for sure is that the darkest room ever, which was being controlled by fear and panic—the Eleven having just witnessed the most gruesome death of all time—was about to become the room where everything changed. It changed because Jesus came, walking into that room where all doors had been shut for the disciples' safety.

Then, the same day at evening, being the first day of the week,
*when the **doors were shut** where the disciples were assembled,*

for fear of the Jews, Jesus came and stood in the midst, and said to them, "Peace be with you." When He had said this, He showed them His hands and His side. Then the disciples were glad when they saw the Lord. So Jesus said to them again, "Peace to you! As the Father has sent Me, I also send you." And when He had said this, He breathed on them, and said to them, "Receive the Holy Spirit. If you forgive the sins of any, they are forgiven them; if you retain the sins of any, they are retained."

(John 20:19–23 NKJV)

I'm sure that when Jesus suddenly arrived, it didn't help the disciples with their fear issues. They were already terrified. Notice they didn't immediately recognize Him, which had to have added to the terror of the moment. Jesus had to show them the scars from the wounds on His hands and side for them to know who He was. The phenomenon of Jesus's appearance being different from what it was when they knew Him in His earthly form before His death is seen a number of times throughout the post-resurrection story. And Jesus continues to manifest Himself to us in various ways to this day. But when He does manifest, it is always in a way consistent with Scripture and never in violation of the Holy Spirit's nature and ways. To this point, we must study the Word of God and become tenderly familiar with and connected to the Spirit of God, who always reveals the Father's heart.

Overflow: The darkest room ever, which was being controlled by fear and panic, was about to become the room where everything changed.

Readings: John 14:27; 16:33

Reflection: Have you been living in a "dark room" of fear or worry? Ask Jesus to enter that room and bring you His peace.

_____

_____

_____

_____

_____

_____

_____

_____

_____

_____

_____

_____

_____

_____

_____

_____

_____

_____

DAY 10

A DAY OF NEW BEGINNINGS

"Then the dove came to him in the evening, and behold,
a freshly plucked olive leaf was in her mouth."
—Genesis 8:11 (NKJV)

In the New Testament, the Holy Spirit takes center stage—nothing happens without Him. On the other hand, the Old Testament provides some of the richest *insights* into the Holy Spirit. The Spirit's nature and heart become obvious in the Old Testament's graphic illustrations of His presence and works. For example, the presence of the Holy Spirit is manifested and symbolized in unique forms in the book of Genesis. In some ways, my favorite illustration from that book is connected to the great man Noah. Noah was commanded to build an ark, a very large boat that would sustain the lives of both human beings and animals during the great flood that was to come upon the earth. Noah's obedience to build the ark and find refuge in it with his family was followed by forty days and nights of rain, until the whole earth was flooded. (See Genesis 6–7.)

Noah waited inside the ark until he knew it was time to obey the next steps in God's plan. He knew it was the right time by "testing the waters." (See Genesis 8:8–12.) In this beautiful story, Noah used a dove to find out if the floodwaters had receded enough that he and his family could leave the boat and start life on land again. When the dove found no resting place, she returned to the ark. Noah seemed to have a personal connection with this dove because the emphasis is on the fact that he *"drew her into the ark to himself."* He waited seven days and then tried again. This time, the dove returned after having been gone for a good part of the day. When she came back, she had an olive leaf in her mouth. That, of course, was a sign that the waters were receding, vegetation was growing again, and it wouldn't be long before Noah and his family could leave the boat. Noah finally released the dove after another seven days of waiting. This time, she did not return again.

The international symbol of peace is an olive branch in the mouth of a dove. This symbol is no doubt taken from this biblical story, which provides us with a profound symbol of peace for the church as well. The dove represents the peace and restoration that the Holy Spirit brings us through Christ.

Because of his obedience, Noah preserved the lives of his family members from the destructive force of the flood that covered the earth. He, his wife, his sons, and his sons' spouses were all saved, as were the lives of those in the animal kingdom that had been brought on board for preservation. Both mankind and the animal kingdom were to repopulate the earth.

In a sense, the earth was being reborn. The evil of the days previous to the flood had reached a maximum level and had to be destroyed. Noah and his children would now have a chance to start over. It was a day of new beginnings.

Overflow: The dove represents the peace and restoration that the Holy Spirit brings us through Christ.

Readings: Genesis 8:8–18; Lamentations 3:22–23

Reflection: What "new beginnings" are you seeking? How might you ask the heavenly Father, through the Holy Spirit, to bring His newness into your life and circumstances?

_____

_____

_____

_____

_____

_____

_____

_____

_____

_____

_____

_____

_____

_____

_____

_____

_____

_____

DAY 11

SOMETHING THAT HAS NEVER EXISTED BEFORE

"Old things have passed away; behold,
all things have become new."
—2 Corinthians 5:17 (NKJV)

When a person is born again, he or she becomes a new creation and is given a brand-new start. *"Therefore, if anyone is in Christ, he is a new creation; old things have passed away; behold, all things have become new"* (2 Corinthians 5:17 NKJV). From the time of the creation of humanity to the time of Christ, there had never been anything newly created—no *new* creation. (Noah was given the opportunity of a new beginning but not of becoming a new creation.) After the sacrificial death and resurrection of Jesus, human beings had the opportunity to be born again by the Spirit of God—the One who raised Christ from the dead. Whenever someone is born again, that person actually becomes something that has never existed before!

Peter describes the phenomenon in this way:

> But **you are a chosen generation, a royal priesthood, a holy nation, His own special people**, that you may proclaim the praises of Him who called you out of darkness into His marvelous light; who once were not a people but **are now the people of God**, who had not obtained mercy but **now have obtained mercy**. (1 Peter 2:9–10 NKJV)

The descriptors of this new creation found in the above passage are simply beautiful. The purpose is equally wonderful: that we may proclaim God's praises!

Peter was "in the room" when this story of the new creation began to unfold. He had witnessed Jesus's crucifixion. (See Luke 23:49.) He was aware of where Jesus's body had been placed in the tomb. (See, for example, Luke 23:55.) He had even seen the empty tomb on the morning of the resurrection. (See John 20:6–9.)

Even though the tomb was empty, Peter and John had no idea at first what that meant for them. Yet this was to become their day of new beginnings. This was to become the day when they discovered the world was completely different from what it had been only a few days earlier. The flood of God's grace had destroyed the powers of darkness that had been killing, stealing, and destroying the lives of humanity ever since Noah was given a clean start. (See John 10:10.) The Holy Spirit living in the disciples would make it possible for them to demonstrate the superior nature of God's kingdom and see it become manifest in practical ways in the lives of broken people.

After the resurrection of Christ, the new day was not marked by an empty earth, about to be repopulated by man and beast. This time, it was—and is—marked by the transformation of individuals from the inside out. That is the best kind of *new day*. The clean canvas was not an earth that was empty of life. The clean canvas was and is the untouched territory called the human heart, ready to be transformed by God's Spirit into the image of Jesus.

⌒

Overflow: The Holy Spirit living in the disciples would make it possible for them to demonstrate the superior nature of God's kingdom and see it become manifest in practical ways in the lives of broken people.

Reading: 2 Corinthians 5:14–20

Reflection: Have you invited the Holy Spirit to transform you into the image of Jesus? Consider writing out your invitation below.

_____

_____

_____

_____

_____

_____

_____

_____

_____

_____

_____

_____

_____

_____

_____

_____

_____

_____

DAY 12

A PLACE TO LAND

"As the Father has sent me, I also send you."
—John 20:21

Before Jesus revealed His identity to the disciples after His resurrection, He told them, *"Peace be with you"* (John 20:19). Imagine with me this moment when Jesus released peace. I think it was much like Noah's releasing of the dove from the ark the first time, when there was nowhere for the dove to land. In Noah's case, the reason was that the floodwaters had not yet receded from the earth. In Jesus's case, the floodwaters of fear had not yet receded from the hearts and minds of the disciples, even though the resurrected One—the One who had defeated death, sin, and all the powers of darkness—was now in the room. If they had recognized the divine moment they were in, they would not have feared anything!

The dove (peace) had not found anywhere to land that was safe. But once Jesus revealed who He was by showing the disciples the scars of His suffering, the flood of fear within them diminished, and the dove now had a place to settle. The Scriptures say, *"Then the disciples were glad when they saw the Lord"* (verse 20). It's quite obvious that they *weren't* glad the first time around! Jesus released the dove again when He said, *"Peace to you!"* (verse 21). This time, He followed the pronouncement of peace with the gift that was to make Noah's day of new beginnings pale in comparison. He breathed on them and said, *"Receive the Holy Spirit"* (verse 22).

Noah received a clean start to a new day, but the disciples *became* the new day: a new creation. As we read earlier, Peter described believers in Jesus as *"a chosen generation, a royal priesthood, a holy nation, His own special people"* (1 Peter 2:9). The same Holy Spirit who hovered over the waters on the day of creation and brought forth all things new (see Genesis 1:2) was now residing in God's people. The Spirit of the resurrected Christ took up residence in them. His blood-bought ones had become the temple of the living God. The dove found not only a safe place to land, but also a place that would honor Him and give Him the rightful position of influence in and through their lives. *Being led by the Spirit* was no longer a pipe dream. It was a reality freely given to all who confessed Jesus as Lord.

One of the parts of this story of the new creation that is both the most challenging and the most inviting to me is Jesus's comment, *"As the Father has sent me, I also send you"* (John 20:21). What was Jesus sent to do? Reveal the Father and release the Holy Spirit. What are we assigned to do? Reveal the Father and release the Holy Spirit.

Overflow: Being led by the Spirit was no longer a pipe dream. It was a reality freely given to all who confessed Jesus as Lord.

Reading: Galatians 5:16–18

Reflection: In what ways are you being led by the Spirit to reveal the heavenly Father and release the Holy Spirit to others who need Him?

_____

_____

_____

_____

_____

_____

_____

_____

_____

_____

_____

_____

_____

_____

_____

_____

_____

_____

DAY 13

IMMERSED IN THE HOLY SPIRIT

"John baptized with water, but you will be baptized with the
Holy Spirit not many days from now."
—Acts 1:5 (NASB)

Jesus gave a specific and essential command to His disciples regarding the Holy Spirit:

> *Gathering them together, He commanded them not to leave*
> *Jerusalem, but to wait for what the Father had promised,*
> *"Which," He said, "you heard of from Me; for John baptized*
> *with water, but **you will be baptized with the Holy Spirit** not*
> *many days from now.... But **you will receive power** when the*
> *Holy Spirit has come upon you; and **you shall be My witnesses***
> *both in Jerusalem, and in all Judea and Samaria, and even to the*
> *remotest part of the earth."*   (Acts 1:4–5, 8 NASB)

It's only with this power from the Holy Spirit that we can give anything close to an accurate representation of (be a witness of) who Jesus is.

While Jesus was on earth, He gave His disciples authority and power to be able to work with Him in His ministry. (See, for example, Luke 9:1–6; 10:1–20.) In a sense, they were deputized to function under His gifts and authority. But when Jesus ascended to heaven, they needed to receive these two graces of authority and power for themselves.

Authority was given to Jesus's followers in the Great Commission. The authority we walk in is equal to our embrace of His mission, into which we are *co-missioned*:

> *And Jesus came up and spoke to them, saying, "**All authority has been given to Me** in heaven and on earth. **Go therefore** and make disciples of all the nations, baptizing them in the name of the Father and the Son and the Holy Spirit, teaching them to observe all that I commanded you; and lo, I am with you always, even to the end of the age."* (Matthew 28:18–20 NASB)

I imagine the disciples had been beside themselves with joy and bewilderment earlier when the resurrected Christ stood before them, giving them instructions to follow for the rest of their lives. (See Luke 24:36–49.) Part of that instruction concerned their mission to go into all the world with the gospel. But Jesus warned them not to fulfill that commission until they had the other grace: power. *"And behold, I am sending forth the promise of My Father upon you; but you are to stay in the city until you are clothed with power from on high"* (Luke 24:49 NASB).

Jesus made it clear that both power and authority are needed to carry out our assignment as His disciples. He made this clear by how He lived and how He trained His disciples in His earthly ministry. And now He reaffirmed this truth in His post-resurrection instructions. It is our responsibility to pursue and receive what God has promised and made available to all believers. Authority comes in the co-mission, while power comes through encounter with the Holy Spirit.

Overflow: Both power and authority are needed to carry out our assignment as Jesus's disciples.

Readings: Luke 24:36–53; Acts 2:1–4

Reflection: How are you pursuing the spiritual power that God has promised and made available to you so that you may carry out Jesus's assignment and represent Him well in the world?

_____

_____

_____

_____

_____

_____

_____

_____

_____

_____

_____

_____

_____

_____

_____

_____

_____

DAY 14

RECEIVING THE SPIRIT OF ADOPTION

"You received the Spirit of adoption by whom we cry out,
"Abba, Father."
—Romans 8:15 (NKJV)

Jesus introduced His disciples to the Spirit of God, who would introduce them further to their heavenly Father, so they could live the corresponding lifestyle they had once observed only in Jesus. This Spirit would lead them as He had led Jesus and continually connect them to Abba Father; He would witness to their spirits that they had been adopted by God and were now joint heirs with Jesus.

The Holy Spirit living within us is the seal of our adoption:

*For as many as are led by the Spirit of God, these are sons of God. For you did not receive the spirit of bondage again to fear, but you received the Spirit of adoption **by whom we cry out, "Abba, Father."** The Spirit Himself bears witness with our spirit that we are children of God, and if children, then heirs—heirs of God and joint heirs with Christ, if indeed we suffer with Him, that we may also be glorified together.*

(Romans 8:14–17 NKJV)

One of the things I enjoy immensely is watching adoption stories on YouTube. They bring me to tears over and over again. The stories often center on a child holding a sign that says something like, "After months of being in foster care and living in five different foster homes, I AM BEING ADOPTED!" The joy on these children's faces—absolute perfection—is worth every sacrifice their adopted families make for such a change in their homes and lifestyles. The joy becomes palpable to me, even though I am watching the scenario unfold on a computer screen.

Multiply these stories by a thousand, and you'll begin to understand the word used to describe our adoption by God. It says we received the Holy Spirit *"by whom we cry out, 'Abba Father.'"* One of the meanings of the Greek word translated as *"cry out"* is "to scream."[2] And the passage says, *"by whom,"* implying that the Holy Spirit is the source of the cry or outburst, affirming our identity by introducing us to our Father. This type of cry would not fit into many people's definition of doing things in the church *"decently and in order"* (1 Corinthians 14:40 NKJV) because it is raw, real, and extreme. But it is from the Holy Spirit, and it is part of our life with this Father! This is a stunning picture of the role of the Holy Spirit: to introduce us to, and strengthen our identity with, the Father.

Jesus's primary role on earth was to reveal the Father. But it wasn't until He released the Holy Spirit that His assignment was complete, for only in the indwelling of the Holy Spirit do we find out who we are because of who our Father is. This is a relational revelation in that we can now personally know the Father, the One so often celebrated by Jesus.

Overflow: It wasn't until Jesus released the Holy Spirit that His assignment to reveal the Father was complete.

Reading: Romans 8:1–17

2. *Strong's*, G2896, Blue Letter Bible Lexicon, https://www.blueletterbible.org/lexicon/g2896/kjv/tr/0-1/.

Reflection: How might you reach out to your Abba Father today, thanking Him for adopting you and making you a beloved member of His family?

_____

_____

_____

_____

_____

_____

_____

_____

_____

_____

_____

_____

_____

_____

_____

_____

_____

DAY 15

THE SPIRIT WITHIN US: OUR INHERITANCE

"The Spirit Himself bears witness with our spirit that we are children of God."
—Romans 8:16 (NKJV)

What does it mean to have God within us? I'm sure you are probably like me in that you're thankful just to be born again. When I hear people say they aren't looking for a reward from God, I get it. Especially when we understand that everything we do that's right, that pleases God, came from Him in the first place. Even our faith, without which we cannot please God (see Hebrews 11:6), came from Him. We obviously play a role in responding to and living for God. But that role is made possible by Him.

Not only that, but He empowers us in everything. Just the thought of being born again, adopted into God's family, is a gift beyond all comprehension. Yet, as only He can do, Jesus pushes the boundary of our comprehension a bit further by adding that we are heirs of God. We inherit God. Astonishing! God, the all-generous and loving One, has given Himself to us. That is what it means to have God within us. *"The Spirit Himself bears witness with our spirit that we are children of God, and if children, then heirs—**heirs of God and joint heirs with Christ**, if indeed we suffer with Him, that we may also be glorified together"* (Romans 8:16–17 NKJV).

In granting this indescribable gift—the Holy Spirit—described as the *"pledge"* (Ephesians 1:14 NASB) or *"down payment"* (AMPC) of this inheritance, God designates there is more to come! He not only gives forgiveness, mercy, grace, blessings, promises, and spiritual gifts galore. He gives us *Himself.*

Waking up to the reality that the presence of the almighty God is not only with us but also dwells in us marks our consciousness in a way that changes everything about our lives.

I am a steward of so much: family, friendships, gifts, insights, opportunities, favor, and about a thousand other things. Each area must be cultivated in reverence and for the glory of God. But there's no greater assignment than stewarding God Himself. He gave Himself to us as an inheritance.

And here's another astonishing truth: God inherits *us!* *"I pray that the eyes of your heart may be enlightened, so that you will know what is the hope of His calling, what are the riches of the glory of **His inheritance in the saints**"* (Ephesians 1:18 NASB). The first chapter of Ephesians is probably the most mind-boggling chapter in the whole Bible for me. And this thought about God inheriting us is on the top of the pile of thoughts revealed there that are beyond our ability to fully comprehend.

We are not some token part of God's creation. We are not His hobby or a side interest. Humanity is not what He dabbles in on the weekends. *We are it.* We are the crowning touch of His creation, which went bad, but which He spent all to redeem. He is "all in"—to the point that He is what we inherit, and we are His inheritance.

〜

Overflow: God not only gives forgiveness, mercy, grace, blessings, promises, and spiritual gifts galore. He gives us *Himself.*

Reading: Ephesians 1

Reflection: After reading this devotion, how would you describe in your own words what it means that God lives within you?

_____

_____

_____

_____

_____

_____

_____

_____

_____

_____

_____

_____

_____

_____

_____

_____

_____

_____

_____

DAY 16

"THIS GLORIOUS TRANSFIGURATION"

*"We are being transfigured into his very image as we move from
one brighter level of glory to another."*
—2 Corinthians 3:18 (TPT)

We have seen that the Holy Spirit is exactly like Jesus; He is referred to as *"another Helper"* in John 14:16 (NASB, NKJV). And we know that Jesus is exactly like the Father. Remember that Jesus told His disciples that if they had seen Him, they had seen the Father. (See John 14:9.) The writer of Hebrews wonderfully expresses this reality:

> *He is the radiance of His glory and **the exact representation of His nature**, and upholds all things by the word of His power. When He had made purification of sins, He sat down at the right hand of the Majesty on high.* (Hebrews 1:3 NASB)

The Holy Spirit is continually making us like Jesus, who is seated at the right hand of the Father in heaven. One of the most mind-boggling scriptural statements in this regard is found in the apostle Paul's second epistle to the church at Corinth:

> *Now the Lord is the Spirit; and **where the Spirit of the Lord is, there is liberty**. But we all, with unveiled face, **beholding as in a mirror the glory of the Lord, are being transformed into***

> *the same image from glory to glory, just as by the Spirit of the
> Lord.* (2 Corinthians 3:17–18 NKJV)

Do you see what this passage is indicating—that we're beholding the glory of the Lord but then discovering we're looking in a mirror? In that mirror, we are seeing the work of the Holy Spirit, who is transforming us *"from glory to glory"* into the image of the glorified Son of God.

Brian Simmons of *The Passion Translation* puts it brilliantly:

> *Now the "Lord" I'm referring to is the Holy Spirit, and wherever
> he is Lord, there is freedom.... We are being transfigured into
> his very image as we move from one brighter level of glory to
> another. And this glorious transfiguration comes from the Lord,
> who is the Spirit.* (2 Corinthians 3:17–18)

We were designed to *host* God, and that interaction with Him is meant to be one of the ways we experience His endless goodness and find our reason for being. Exploring the nature of God is in some ways a discovery of who we are. When the Holy Spirit takes up residence in us, and we are yielded to Him, we naturally mirror the heart and nature of God through our thoughts, attitudes, and actions. The enemy of our souls works hard to tarnish that manifestation of who God is in this world. He does so by trying to persuade us to embrace anxiety, fear, resentment, and regret. Such things lead us down a path that has no answer but repentance. Yielding to God's Word and resisting the devil's plans for us enable us to carry God's presence, nature, and assignment into the earth.

Overflow: When the Holy Spirit takes up residence in us, and we are yielded to Him, we naturally mirror the heart and nature of God through our thoughts, attitudes, and actions.

Reading: 2 Corinthians 3:7–18

Reflection: In what specific ways is the Holy Spirit transforming you into the image of Jesus?

_____

_____

_____

_____

_____

_____

_____

_____

_____

_____

_____

_____

_____

_____

_____

_____

_____

DAY 17

MAINTAINING AN ATMOSPHERE FOR HOSTING

"Therefore, since we are receiving a kingdom which cannot be shaken, let us have grace, by which we may serve God acceptably with reverence and godly fear."
—Hebrews 12:28 (NKJV)

The Holy Spirit being our Helper is all about enabling us to fulfill our purpose and potential as redeemed members of God's family. The heavenly partnership that is available to us is completely carried out in our relationship with Him. This, then, is the pinnacle of God's creation of us as His co-laborers: God Himself dwelling in us, enabling us to step into the fullness of our purpose in Him.

We need to maintain an atmosphere in our lives for hosting God's Spirit. As an illustration of this point, remember that Jesus warned of the eternal consequences of blaspheming the Holy Spirit. He said that we could blaspheme Him or the Father, and that could be forgiven, but there's no forgiveness to those who blaspheme the Holy Spirit. (See, for example, Luke 12:10.) This is an incredible mystery to me, and my purpose is not to alarm you but to emphasize that this picture is clear: the Holy Spirit is revered by the Father and the Son and must be revered by us as well. He must not be violated.

The believer's life is lived best by remembering these two approaches to the Holy Spirit, established by the Father: we are not to grieve the Holy Spirit (see Ephesians 4:30), and we are not to quench the Holy Spirit (see 1 Thessalonians 5:19). We grieve Him with wrong behavior, attitudes, thoughts, and plans. This command is focused on our character. We quench Him when we fail to cooperate with Him, stopping the flow of His Word and His power in our lives. This command is focused on the release of power. These are the two legs we stand on: character and power. And one is not more important than the other.

The Holy Spirit is the delicate One, the One with whom we must exert extra caution and care. And yet it is the Holy Spirit who is assigned to live in us. Think of it: broken, despised, sin-filled humanity becomes the dwelling place of the delicate One. (Forgive me; I'm not sure *delicate* is the best word to use, as it could imply weakness, which, of course, is not the case. But hopefully it's close enough to get the picture.) I say this to emphasize the absolutely successful impact of the blood of Jesus applied to a life, which restores that person to the status of humanity in the garden of Eden before sin: being the dwelling place of God. Another important thought in this regard is that we can tell how much God trusts us by recognizing what He has entrusted to us: He has entrusted us with the Holy Spirit Himself. That act, in itself, reveals God's confidence in the power and effectiveness of the blood of Jesus in our lives.

Overflow: This is the pinnacle of God's creation of us as His co-laborers: God Himself dwelling in us, enabling us to step into the fullness of our purpose in Him.

Readings: Ephesians 4:29–32; 1 Thessalonians 5:19–22

Reflection: Take time for some personal evaluation with regard to your hosting of the Holy Spirit: Are there any ways in which you might be grieving Him by your attitudes or actions? Are there any ways in which you might be quenching His power by not cooperating with the flow of His work in your life? If so, repent for these attitudes and actions and receive Jesus's forgiveness and a fresh start in your relationship with the Holy Spirit.

DAY 18

A REALM OF FREEDOM

"If the Son makes you free, you will be free indeed."
—John 8:36 (NASB)

In the mystery of the Godhead, God the Father is upon His throne in heaven, the Son of God is seated at His right hand, and the Holy Spirit is God on earth, living in His eternal dwelling place, His temple: God's people. The Holy Spirit is the One who enables us to succeed in all the Father has assigned us to be and do. As we come to know the Spirit, we will enter into a deeper relationship with Him.

Again, the Holy Spirit takes us *"from glory to glory"* (2 Corinthians 3:18 NKJV, NASB). And we are to anticipate receiving this "more" because this is His heart for us: "[Jesus] *said, 'To you it has been granted to know the mysteries of the kingdom of God'"* (Luke 8:10 NASB). It is the Holy Spirit who is the Revealer of truth to us all: *"But when He, the Spirit of truth, comes, He will guide you into all the truth; for He will not speak on His own initiative, but whatever He hears, He will speak; and He will disclose to you what is to come"* (John 16:13 NASB).

What I have learned from years of experience and studying the Scriptures is that the Holy Spirit is expert at listening without reacting, kind in His responses, genuine—never artificial—and honest in a way that serves us well while also setting us free from inferior things in our lives without bringing us shame. He continues to welcome us even when we fall short, when we go to Him in fear, anger, resentment, or unbelief. However, He also has no tolerance for sin, which is anything that is contrary to His holy and loving nature. He has no intention of giving us an "audience with the King" yet allowing us to leave the same way we entered. Knowing Him changes us. Completely. Perhaps I should put it this way: under such circumstances, if we leave our time of prayer in the same manner in which we came to it, we weren't praying—we were complaining.

The Holy Spirit always works to bring us into His realm of freedom. In fact, it can be said that the amount of influence He has in a person's life is measured by the freedom in which they live. The Spirit manifests the Prince of Peace. He is always present, never distracted, and never too busy for us. He values faith more than we realize because, as God, He is the most trustworthy one in existence. Our faith in Him is powerful only because of His perfect trustworthiness. When we consider God's nature of complete faithfulness, faith is our only reasonable response.

⌣

Overflow: The Holy Spirit always works to bring us into His realm of freedom.

Reading: Romans 6:20–22

Reflection: From what has Christ set you free? What aspects of your freedom in Christ do you need to enter into more fully?

_____

_____

_____

_____

_____

_____

_____

_____

_____

_____

_____

_____

_____

_____

_____

_____

_____

_____

_____

_____

DAY 19

THE SPIRIT OF HOLINESS

"Oh, worship the LORD in the beauty of holiness!"
—Psalm 96:9 (NKJV)

If the Holy Spirit were to have His way, what would the church look like? Like Jesus. Pure and simple. It is for this reason that we are called *"the body of Christ."* (See, for example, 1 Corinthians 12:27.) Jesus is joyful beyond description, is abundantly filled with life, and delights in the wonder of His Father while being perfectly united with the Holy Spirit, who dwells in His people. He skillfully reigns over all things in a way that brings joy to His Father. He is perfect in beauty, in wonder, and in majesty. Around the throne is the continuous decree *"Holy, holy, holy"* (Isaiah 6:3; Revelation 4:8)! Apparently, holiness is a dominant theme of His person, His being. Of all the things that could be declared, such as His worth, His beauty, or His love, it is His holiness that is proclaimed throughout eternity.

The Bible speaks of *"the beauty of holiness."* (See, for example, Psalm 29:2.) Most of us have been exposed to and/or frustrated by the religious idea of holiness, which is more like self-righteousness or adherence to rules and regulations. As a result, holiness is thought of as restrictive and rigid. Yet true holiness is the heart of freedom. We may think we are free when we are living fully according to our own design and purpose, but we are never freer than when we are living a holy life. Such a life is called "beautiful." Here is the perfect description of *holiness*: "the essence of beauty."

It's tragic to see *unholiness* paraded as *beauty*. It must delight the enemy of our souls to see people fall for the counterfeit. All of the devil's rewards come with a balloon payment. In other words, you can have a reward (pleasure) now, but it will cost you when you least expect it. Partnering with the enemy's works and ways positions us to live in his debt forever. Holiness is the opposite of that. It is permanent freedom because it is anchored in the nature and person of God.

Isn't it interesting that the writer of Hebrews declares, *"Pursue peace with all people, and holiness, without which no one will see the Lord"* (Hebrews 12:14 NKJV)? We'd all be doomed if this required a holiness that was in and of ourselves. But our relationship of surrender to Jesus through the Holy Spirit gives Him the place of influence over our lives to the point that His nature is seen in and through us. He is the *Holy* Spirit. He is the Spirit of Holiness. Responding to His influence is the only possible way for us to live in and experience the holiness of God flowing through our lives.

Overflow: We are never freer than when we are living a holy life.

Reading: Psalm 96

Reflection: Why is holiness "permanent freedom"? In what ways have you found holiness to be freeing?

_____

_____

_____

_____

_____

_____

_____

_____

_____

_____

_____

_____

_____

_____

_____

_____

_____

_____

_____

DAY 20

FRUIT OF THE SPIRIT: CHARACTER TRANSFORMED

"But the fruit of the Spirit is love, joy, peace, patience, kindness, goodness, faithfulness, gentleness, self-control."
—Galatians 5:22–23 (NASB)

The abiding presence of God always has an impact on the thought life, behavior, and character of a person. The fruit, or effects, of the Holy Spirit's working in an individual are measurable. They are the evidence of grace at work in the child of God. One of the major differences between law and grace is that law *requires* while grace *enables*. The indwelling presence of God, through grace, brings about change from the inside out. Religious cultures—in the negative sense of those that embrace form without power, and ritual without relationship—also require change of their members. But such change is always from the outside in. In other words, it's related to what people can accomplish through human effort, discipline, and determination. In those cultures, the incentive to bring about change often comes through group thought or peer pressure.

In saying this, I don't want to cast a negative light on personal discipline, which is such an important part of our lives. It's just that self-effort cannot change the nature of a person. Only the grace of God, through the indwelling presence of the Holy Spirit, can bring about a transformational experience. This transformation is absolutely necessary because it enables and equips us to represent Jesus well.

The apostle Paul described this effect in his epistle to the church at Galatia:

> *But the fruit of the [Holy] Spirit [the work which His presence within accomplishes] is love, joy (gladness), peace, patience (an even temper, forbearance), kindness, goodness (benevolence), faithfulness, gentleness (meekness, humility), self-control (self-restraint, continence). Against such things there is no law [that can bring a charge]. And those who belong to Christ Jesus (the Messiah) have crucified the flesh (the godless human nature) with its passions and appetites and desires. If we live by the [Holy] Spirit, let us also walk by the Spirit. [If by the Holy Spirit we have our life in God, let us go forward walking in line, our conduct controlled by the Spirit.] Let us not become vainglorious and self-conceited, competitive and challenging and provoking and irritating to one another, envying and being jealous of one another.* (Galatians 5:22–26 AMPC)

The first thing to note about this passage is that when all these virtues are listed—*love, joy, peace, patience, kindness, goodness, faithfulness, gentleness,* and *self-control*—they are mentioned as only one fruit. Singular. They are not called the "fruits" of the Holy Spirit. That amazes me in so many ways. It's also extremely encouraging to see that whenever God is dealing with us in a specific area, His transforming work will touch every area of our lives, all at the same time. In other words, He's not just trying to make me more patient, but He is trying to make me kinder or more joyful (or any of the other qualities listed) at the same time. All the virtues are interrelated.

⌒

Overflow: Only the grace of God, through the indwelling presence of the Holy Spirit, can bring about a transformational experience.

Reading: Mark 4:13–20

Reflection: Which aspects of the fruit of the Spirit do you see evident in your life? Which do you feel especially need more growth and development?

_____

_____

_____

_____

_____

_____

_____

_____

_____

_____

_____

_____

_____

_____

_____

_____

_____

_____

PART TWO:

FILLED

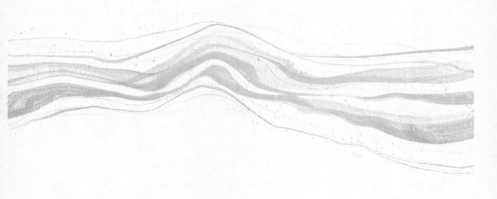

DAY 21

ALL THE FULLNESS OF GOD

"That you may be filled up to all the fullness of God."
—Ephesians 3:19 (NASB)

Because we were made in God's image, everything about us—spirit, soul, and body—is perfectly suited for a relationship with Him. Even our physical body, with its senses, was intended to help us experience and come to know Him. We were given this design so that we can feel and enjoy God's presence. Our senses can be trained to recognize what is from God, in contrast to what is not from God and is therefore wrong or lesser in value. (See Hebrews 5:14.)

Our relationship with the Holy Spirit is what clarifies God's purposes for us and enables us to live in the center of the mind of Christ. Growing in our understanding of God has even greater importance when we realize that *insight is meant to lead to encounter.* Whatever knowledge about God we receive should lead to a deeper relationship with Him. The secret to real knowing is therefore the knowing of the heart.

Ephesians 3 assures us we can know what is beyond knowing. In other words, our heart can take us where our head can't "fit." Paul's prayer for believers in this verse is quite challenging: that we would *"know the love of Christ which surpasses knowledge, that [we] may be filled up to all the fullness of God"* (Ephesians 3:19 NASB). This petition points to an astounding invitation. We can experience that which surpasses knowledge, but it doesn't stop there. The conclusion of this incomprehensible statement is *"that you may be filled up to all the fullness of God."* Really? Filled with the fullness of God Himself? He fills the galaxies, holding every molecule in place through the power of His word. (See Colossians 1:17; Hebrews 1:3.) And this God has determined to *fill us* with His fullness? The surrender that leads to encounter paves the way for experiencing such extravagance.

The *Amplified* translation brings out the beauty of Ephesians 3:19 in a unique way:

> And [that you may come] to know [practically, **through personal experience**] the love of Christ which far surpasses [mere] knowledge [without experience], that you may be filled up [throughout your being] to **all the fullness of God** [so that you may have the richest experience of God's presence in your lives, **completely filled and flooded with God Himself**].

Could there be a greater promise than being *"completely filled and flooded with God Himself"*? I can't imagine what that could be! The concept of being filled with God is generally described with this phrase: "filled with the Holy Spirit." The Spirit is the One who fills us. In a very real sense, we were designed to contain and host the Holy Spirit Himself.

Overflow: Insight is meant to lead to encounter.

Reading: Ephesians 3:14–21

Reflection: What insights about God have you have received that have led you to encounter Him in a personal way?

_____

_____

_____

_____

_____

_____

_____

_____

_____

_____

_____

_____

_____

_____

_____

_____

_____

_____

DAY 22

BE FILLED

"Do not be drunk with wine,...but be filled with the Spirit."
—Ephesians 5:18 (NKJV)

My personal favorite description of the Holy Spirit's work in and through someone is found in the story of Gideon in Judges 6:34. Some Bible translations state that the Spirit of God came "on" or "upon" Gideon. But the wording in the original Hebrew seems dramatically different from this. It states that "the Holy Spirit clothed Himself with Gideon."[3]

While I love this Old Testament story of the Holy Spirit working through Gideon, there's no way that Gideon's anointing could have been superior to what God has promised and made available to all who are *filled with the Holy Spirit* under the new covenant. Superior blessings never come from inferior covenants. What is available to us now is greater than what Gideon had—and we must pursue it. That means that the wonder and beauty of Gideon's experience are surpassed in the life of every believer who is truly filled with the Holy Spirit.

Sometimes we become so familiar with a truth that we are no longer impressed or even impacted by it. Having the Holy Spirit dwelling in us seems to be one of those realities. Consider again this thought: in Ephesians 3:19 (NKJV), Paul says that we are to be *"filled*

---

3. *NKJV Spirit-Filled Life Bible* (Nashville, TN: Thomas Nelson, 1991), 357.

with all the fullness of God." As I mentioned before, I'm not sure that there is a more incomprehensible idea than that one! God is everywhere, all at once. The mere size of the eternal One is immeasurable. And that One wants to fill us *with His fullness.* Once more, these are not ideas to comprehend. They are to be embraced with the heart and considered as invitations to a deeper relationship with Him and a greater awareness of our design and purpose. Through surrender to the beauty of such mysteries, let's come under the influence of truths beyond the reach of human intellect or emotional capacity.

Another statement about this fullness is found in Ephesians 5:18 (NKJV): *"Do not be drunk with wine,...but be filled with the Spirit."* I have heard Randy Clark, the great author, revivalist, and international speaker, brilliantly expound on the meaning of this verse. He reminds us that wine has no effect on a person while it is in a bottle. It still has no effect when it is in a glass. It must get from the glass to the stomach of an individual to have its intoxicating effect. The lesson here is not complicated. When something is in you, it has an effect. *"Be filled with the Spirit"* is not a suggestion. It is a command: live under the "intoxicating" influence of the Holy Spirit.

The bottom line is that when the Holy Spirit takes up residence in us, all of heaven expects there to be results *in* us (character) and *through* us (in the supernatural and natural gifts we exercise to express Him well). The very presence of God in a person makes the impossibilities of life possible.

⌒

Overflow: *"Be filled with the Spirit"* is not a suggestion. It is a command.

Reading: Ephesians 5:8–18

Reflection: How do you respond to the command *"Be filled with the Spirit"*?

_____

_____

_____

_____

_____

_____

_____

_____

_____

_____

_____

_____

_____

_____

_____

_____

DAY 23

CONTINUOUSLY FILLED

"Speaking to one another in psalms and hymns and spiritual songs, singing and making melody with your heart to the Lord."
—Ephesians 5:19 (NASB)

In the Greek, the words in Ephesians 5:18 translated *"be filled"* are in the present imperative tense, which means that we are to be in a continuous and ongoing state of being filled with the Holy Spirit.[4] Keeping ourselves in such a place enables us to serve well both in and out of season (see 2 Timothy 4:2), with both authority and power, often accomplishing great things without even trying. This kind of lifestyle will sometimes allow the person on whom the Spirit rests to see more miracles happen "by accident" than they ever did while purposefully seeking them.

In discussing the meaning of Ephesians 5:18, Ché Ahn explains that it indicates, "Be continually filled with the fullness of the Holy Spirit."[5] I love that. Be continuously filled with the Holy Spirit's fullness. Being continuously filled impacts the people we minister to, but it also affects our own thinking about, attitude toward, and hope for any present impossibilities in our lives. Our confidence level in God

4. "What Does It Mean 'Be Filled with the Spirit'?", A Series on the Holy Spirit—Baptism Versus Filling: Part 4, http://helpmewithbiblestudy.org/3HolySpirit/DefBeFilled.aspx.
5. Ché Ahn, "How to Stay Continually Filled and Overflowing in the Holy Spirit," October 21, 2019, The Passion Translation, https://www.thepassiontranslation.com/how-to-stay-continually-filled-and-overflowing-in-the-holy-spirit/.

soars to an all-time high when we live in an awareness of *Emmanuel, God with us.* (See Matthew 1:23.) Another way to state this is that whatever becomes an ongoing feast for our souls overflows into a feast for all those under our influence.

Of course, Jesus first modeled this lifestyle. He was continuously filled with the Spirit. He often went to a mountain to pray—sometimes all night. Here is a reminder on how to stay filled: keep consciously before God in worship and prayer. *"Rejoice always; pray without ceasing; in everything give thanks"* (1 Thessalonians 5:16–18 NASB). This approach to life keeps us continually before God with joy, engaging with Him regarding every issue of life, giving Him thanks and praise in the midst of difficulty and mystery. It keeps us under His constant influence.

In the natural world, being full usually means being satisfied. In the kingdom, it's the opposite. The most spiritually hungry people I know are those who are the greatest at living a lifestyle of being unceasingly filled with the Holy Spirit. They are in constant pursuit of the more of God. There is always more. And only the childlike can see it and pursue it, sometimes with reckless abandon. Perhaps this is what Paul was talking about when he said to *"pursue love, yet desire earnestly spiritual gifts"* (1 Corinthians 14:1 NASB). This is an aggressive, focused, and intentional pursuit of having the realities of the Holy Spirit's nature and abilities flow through us for the betterment of the people around us. The Spirit wonderfully overflows from our lives, not only to believers, but also to those who don't yet know Christ.

Overflow: To stay filled with the Holy Spirit, keep consciously before God in worship and prayer.

Reading: Ephesians 5:19–20

Reflection: How might you begin to integrate "rejoicing always, praying without ceasing, giving thanks in everything, and singing and making melody with your heart to the Lord" throughout your day today? How might you develop this as a daily habit?

_____

_____

_____

_____

_____

_____

_____

_____

_____

_____

_____

_____

_____

_____

_____

_____

DAY 24

HEAVENLY SEARCH ENGINE

"The Spirit searches all things, yes, the deep things of God."
—1 Corinthians 2:10 (NKJV)

The greatest "search engine" in the universe is the Holy Spirit. And the greatest reservoir of information and insight is the mind of God, which is, in itself, eternal and unlimited in scope and ever-expanding. The Holy Spirit searches the Father's mind, looking for specific thoughts that will conform us more closely to the likeness of Jesus, with greater strength and faith. Merely increasing our self-confidence is never the goal, as the "self" provides very limited progress, if any. But when we receive the revelation of God's mind for us, we find out who we are and who He has made us to be. Just learning His thoughts about us is liberating. We discover our true selves, as we are in Christ, in the revelation of who God is. And that is our strength.

The apostle Paul addresses this theme in a letter to the church of Corinth:

> But as it is written: "Eye has not seen, nor ear heard, nor have entered into the heart of man the things which God has prepared for those who love Him." But God has revealed them to us through His Spirit. For the Spirit searches all things, yes, the deep things of God. For what man knows the things of a man except the spirit of the man which is in him? Even so no one

knows the things of God except the Spirit of God. Now we have received, not the spirit of the world, but the Spirit who is from God, that we might know the things that have been freely given to us by God. (1 Corinthians 2:9–12 NKJV)

The first thing to take note of in this passage is the statement in verse 9 that what God has prepared for us has never even entered our minds. Not even in our wildest and most extreme dreams have we ever approached the wonder and beauty of what God has created for us. Paul then says that God has revealed these things *through His Spirit.* What has always been beyond the reach of human intellect and imagination is now within reach of anyone who learns to hear the voice of the Holy Spirit. You've heard the phrase "It's too good to be true." In our case, "It's so good, it must be true."

The Holy Spirit is the agent of mystery, introducing us to our eternal purpose of discovering the things of God that have already been given to us by inheritance. The Spirit is constantly trying to help us to receive and utilize our inheritance, which becomes manifest in greater measure every time He speaks. He always works in us for the glory of God.

Overflow: What has always been beyond the reach of human intellect and imagination is now within reach of anyone who learns to hear the voice of the Holy Spirit.

Reading: Psalm 139:17–18

Reflection: What are some insights beyond your own intellect and imagination that God has revealed to you? How have they transformed your outlook on and response to life?

_____

_____

_____

_____

_____

_____

_____

_____

_____

_____

_____

_____

_____

_____

_____

_____

_____

_____

DAY 25

FREEDOM AS A LIFESTYLE

"It was for freedom that Christ set us free."
—Galatians 5:1 (NASB)

As much as I like the idea of every believer becoming an instrument in God's hand to bring freedom to others, in order to do this, each of us has to first experience freedom and cultivate it as a lifestyle. The goal is that being led by the Spirit, being empowered by the Spirit, being set free by the Spirit in our personal lives will open up a way of living in us that forever exposes the inferior nature of every other lifestyle. It will position us to love and serve others authentically—genuinely and with authority. Anytime we serve people out of a place of experience in God, we serve with authority.

We must remember that surrender to God leads the way to personal freedom. Like most everything in the kingdom of God, this seems to be a paradox. In this great lesson, we surrender control of our lives to the Holy Spirit, who then teaches us self-control. We yield our ways to God's complete dominion, only to find that's the place where we are the most free. Free to think and feel without restraint. Creating such a culture of freedom doesn't mean that "anything goes." Being restrained by God from fleshly lifestyles actually leads us to the greatest place of living without restraint.

Many church cultures use intimidation and manipulation in their tool set to get people to do the right thing. I think this approach often comes from a desire to motivate people to serve the Lord with all of their hearts. But it usually comes from leaders who have never learned how the kingdom of God actually works.

Whether it's in the church or our homes, living in freedom is necessary for us to become all that God intended. Our development is stunted in a controlling culture. For example, a fish in captivity will only grow to the size its fish tank can support. A shark that will grow to eight feet in length in open waters will grow to no more than eight inches in the average fish tank. Religious cultures will shout and celebrate the eight-inch shark for its beauty and swiftness, often ignorant that God designed the shark to be eight feet long. Only freedom—the kind the Holy Spirit brings—creates the room for that kind of development.

When the church I serve began to significantly increase in number, the staff asked me how we were to build a big church. They were interested in how to construct a large ministry. I told them I wasn't interested in building a big ministry—I just wanted to build *big people*. For me, big people are not those with the biggest titles. They are the freest ones: free from their past, free to fulfill personal dreams, and free to give themselves generously to those under their influence.

⌣‿‿‿〉

Overflow: Surrender to God leads the way to personal freedom.

Reading: James 1:23–25

Reflection: In what ways has your freedom in Christ impacted you in the practical matters of life? How might you further cultivate this freedom as a lifestyle?

_____

_____

_____

_____

_____

_____

_____

_____

_____

_____

_____

_____

_____

_____

_____

_____

_____

DAY 26

PROSPERING IN ALL THINGS

"He shall be like a tree planted by the rivers of water,
that brings forth its fruit in its season…;
and whatever he does shall prosper."
—Psalm 1:3 (NKJV)

When the Holy Spirit lives in us, prosperity of soul is the initial target of His influence. His presence must have a significant impact on our inner world. Let's face it: we have seen that having more money without also having inner health is a nightmare situation. News reports are filled with the tragic stories of those who seemingly "had it all" but overdosed on drugs or killed themselves because it wasn't enough to satisfy them. So, I am not speaking about prosperity according to how our culture usually defines it. There remains a biblical pattern of prosperity that is meant to influence every part of our lives:

> Beloved, **I pray that you may prosper in all things** and be in health, just as your soul prospers. (3 John 1:2 NKJV)

The Holy Spirit-inspired prayer recorded in this verse reveals the will of God: prosperity in every area of life, overflowing into physical health. The fact that such prosperity must be prayed for shows us that this way of living is not necessarily automatic. This desire of the Lord for us must be apprehended in prayer and lived out through a relationship with the Holy Spirit. We know that wherever the Holy Spirit demonstrates the lordship of Jesus, liberty is the result. This freedom is first an inner-man experience, where sin, regret, resentment, shame, guilt, anxiety, comparison, and other negative aspects no longer have a voice or a place of influence in us. Our inner health becomes a stronghold of peace.

When the emotional and mental world of a person is healthy, it affects every other area of their life, from their physical health, to the realms of creativity (free thinking), to wise decision-making, to their financial well-being. For this reason, this prayer in 3 John acknowledges that every part of our life can prosper and be abundant if our soul prospers. At Bethel Church, we have many teams whose primary focus is on ministering healing to the inner man. They testify to the fact that physical healing often follows inner healing.

Psalm 1:3 reads, *"Whatever he does shall prosper,"* and 3 John 1:2 reads, *"That you may prosper in all things."* Both verses reveal the results when the Holy Spirit has a great influence in a person's life. The subject of prosperity triggers many people who feel the need to react negatively to this biblical truth. Of course, their reasoning is in reaction to the abuses of some. I get it. But reaction to error often creates another error. Prosperity can be a result of the influence of the Spirit of God in a person's life. This concept is in the Bible, in the Old and New Testaments alike. It's our responsibility to find out the purpose of His blessing and use it accordingly.

Overflow: When the Holy Spirit lives in us, prosperity of soul is the initial target of His influence.

Reading: 1 Thessalonians 5:23–24

Reflection: What is the biblical pattern of prosperity? How have you seen this pattern evidenced in your life?

_____

_____

_____

_____

_____

_____

_____

_____

_____

_____

_____

_____

_____

_____

_____

_____

_____

DAY 27

AN ENLARGED HEART

*"I will run the course of Your commandments,
for You shall enlarge my heart."*
—Psalm 119:32 (NKJV)

As I look back over my life, I would have to say that my commitment to minister to God as a priest (according to Exodus 19:6 and 1 Peter 2:9) in thanksgiving, praise, and worship was one of the most important covenants I have ever made. It was in response to my dad's teaching on Ezekiel 44:15–31, where the priests were instructed on how to minister in the inner court (to God) and the outer court (to people). It truly changed my life by giving me an understanding of our original design as New Testament believers.

In our ministry to God, we attend to Him. He's not an egotist in need of our affirmation, but because we always become like the one whom we worship, God could want nothing better for us than to become like Him. That's what love does: it chooses the best. This explains why God looks for worshippers, not worship itself.

God's presence comes so powerfully during such times of ministry. David taught us that God inhabits the praises of His people. (See Psalm 22:3 KJV.) It's as though our praise becomes the throne that He sits upon. It is in His presence that we learn to receive, to give, and, above all, to recognize Him. The Holy Spirit is really the One who leads all true worship because those who truly worship God *worship Him in spirit and in truth.* (See John 4:23–24.)

Those who long for God see Him more easily than those who are waiting for Him to invade their space and make Himself overtly obvious. Hunger sees. Faith sees.

Affection for God is a vital expression, and it comes from having an enlarged heart. *"I will run the course of Your commandments, for **You shall enlarge my heart**"* (Psalm 119:32 NKJV). Having an enlarged heart is the ever-increasing capacity to recognize God with delight and do whatever He says. In this place of intimate connection, we learn the ways of divine affection. We are shaped by our time in the glory, which is the manifest presence of Jesus.

In this place of affection, an understanding of spiritual things is awakened in us that has often lain dormant for our whole lives. It's not until we enter the realms of God's glorious presence that we discover the atmosphere we were designed to live in. Our inner man sees it clearly and responds with surrender.

Affection leads us to *adoration*, which is a more biblical term than affection. Adoration is at the heart and soul of true worship. One of the Greek words for *worship* means "to kiss," which clearly emphasizes the intimate connection we were born for.

To offer adoration means to be captivated by the One. To ascend the hill of the Lord with all of life laid down. Time stops. Problems cease. Nothing matters but His heart. Surrendering, pursuing, drawing nearer to the Lord. This is the life of the lover of God.

Overflow: God looks for worshippers, not worship itself.

Reading: Psalm 119:26–32

Reflection: In what ways have you longed for God and been captivated by Him? How will you offer Him adoration today?

_____

_____

_____

_____

_____

_____

_____

_____

_____

_____

_____

_____

_____

_____

_____

_____

_____

_____

DAY 28

A PRICELESS CHALLENGE

"'For who is he who will devote himself to be close to me?'
declares the LORD."
—Jeremiah 30:21 (NIV)

Imagine a billionaire coming to you with a challenge. He has in his possession a ring with the rarest of diamonds in its setting, valued at fifty million dollars. The billionaire has this offer: You have to wear the ring for six months without ever taking it off. You can't even remove it to shower. If you are successful in wearing and caring for this ring, you get to keep it. If you somehow lose it, you are indebted to the man for the sum of fifty million dollars. You would lose everything you own. Do you accept the challenge? Most of us would undoubtedly say yes.

So now, if you accept the challenge, let me ask you this: When you wake up in the morning, are you mindful of the ring? When you shower, are you conscious of what's on your finger? When you are out to dinner, are you aware of the ring? Most people would say, "Yes, yes, yes."

The same would be true of me. I would always be aware of this extremely valuable ring. I wouldn't be able to ignore it or forget it. And I doubt the novelty would wear off in ninety days or even six months. Perhaps five years of wearing the ring would create a neglectful familiarity with it. But not six months. And yet we have One living inside us who is more valuable and more glorious and obvious than all the wealth in the world. To live unaware of Him is a tragic waste of the potential for connection with God and the activation of affection toward Him.

It's usually only those who have breathing issues who live with an awareness of every breath they take. There's such labor involved that they can't help it. But those who have healthy lungs and breathe normally seldom give a thought to what is natural for us all. Our breathing happens every moment of every day, even while we sleep. I don't consciously think about the fact that I have been breathing all day and all night, and yet I have been.

Similarly, the Holy Spirit's presence is constant. He never leaves. But it is possible, and actually common, for us to live *within reach* of this One but still be *unaware* of Him. For me, my strength in my relationship with the Holy Spirit is my affection for Him. If I consider Him, His nearness, and His nature, my heart burns for Him.

Brother Lawrence wrote the classic book *The Practice of the Presence of God*. In it, he describes his journey to live with a consciousness of the Holy Spirit's presence every moment of every day. And while, by his own admittance, he never achieved perfection in this area, he did constantly improve in it. He finally got to the place where being aware of Him while washing the pots and pans was as deep an encounter and fellowship with God as when he was in the chapel praying.

Overflow: We have One living inside us who is more valuable and more glorious and obvious than all the wealth in the world.

Reading: Jeremiah 30:18–22

Reflection: What do you think about the billionaire's challenge? How would you respond to it? How does the diamond ring in the story compare to God's Spirit living within you?

_____

_____

_____

_____

_____

_____

_____

_____

_____

_____

_____

_____

_____

_____

_____

_____

_____

_____

DAY 29

VALUING MYSTERY

*"We declare God's wisdom, a mystery that has been hidden and
that God destined for our glory before time began."*
—1 Corinthians 2:7 (NIV)

Even though our knowledge and understanding of God is always
to be increasing, we can never fully comprehend Him. We will keep
learning more about Him throughout eternity. Here's the very
unusual reality we live in: while our knowledge of God increases, the
mystery of Him increases all the more. It is vital for us to live in this
tension in order to enter into all that He has purposed for us in this
life.

Valuing the quality of mystery will help us keep the fear of the
Lord intact in our lives, while making this relational journey with
Him a continual adventure. If I only obey what I understand, I have
reduced God to my size. I have fashioned a god in my own image.
Mystery surrounding God is essential, if for no other reason than
to prompt us to prove we trust Him even though we can't understand everything about Him. While understanding more about God
brings us awe and celebration, increased mystery about Him gives us
the opportunity to trust Him in our divine partnership with Him.
Mysteries are wonderful opportunities to exercise the divine percep-
tions of the heart.

In considering our relationship with our Creator, let's keep this very important biblical concept in mind: *we can know by experience what is beyond mental comprehension.* Again those who develop a relationship with God through their natural understanding alone only end up with a god in their own image. It's supposed to be the other way around: we are created in the image of God; and, in Christ, we are being changed *"from glory to glory"* (2 Corinthians 3:18 NKJV, NASB) as we are exposed to God's manifest presence and yield to His glory, power, and will. Our thinking changes the more we understand and discover Him.

Our relationship with God has to originate, function, and grow through our spirit, or our heart. The heart is the place from which our faith flows. The Word says, *"With the heart one believes unto righteousness"* (Romans 10:10 NKJV). Not with the mind. The mind has to be trained to perceive correctly through a surrendered heart. Since the heart is the place of faith, it is only right that a relationship with the Holy Spirit comes from the heart. Great faith grows through our yielding, not our striving. That is how a relationship with God is nurtured: Surrendering. Yielding.

Only through surrender can we embark on and progress in this journey to know the One who is beyond knowing, from a natural standpoint. Having the mind of Christ is included in the inheritance of the believer. (See 1 Corinthians 2:16.) When our mind isn't under the Spirit's influence, it opposes God. But under the influence of the Holy Spirit, our mind is the perfect partner and co-laborer with God. There is no neutral ground.

⌒

Overflow: Only through surrender can we embark on and progress in this journey to know the One who is beyond knowing, from a natural standpoint.

Reading: 1 Corinthians 2:13–16

Reflection: What does it mean for you to live in the tension between your knowledge of God and the continued or increased mystery about Him? How can the mystery surrounding God be an opportunity for you to trust Him?

_____

_____

_____

_____

_____

_____

_____

_____

_____

_____

_____

_____

_____

_____

_____

_____

_____

_____

_____

_____

DAY 30

THE ESSENCE OF KINGDOM REASONING

*"Abraham reasoned that God could even raise the dead, and so
in a manner of speaking he did receive Isaac back from death."*
—Hebrews 11:19 (NIV)

Although the Holy Spirit is mysterious by nature because He is
Spirit, we must realize that since He is God, He is also the essence
of practicality and reasonableness. But be forewarned: His is the reasoning of another world, one much superior to ours in every way. A
comprehension of such reasoning is usually found where there is a
willing heart, not just a curious mind. The Roman centurion whose
story is found in Matthew 8:5–13 wonderfully illustrates this truth.
He was outside of the house of Israel and had no obvious spiritual
training, but his understanding of spiritual authority stunned even
the Master Himself, Jesus. My point is this: if a Roman centurion can
get it, so can we. It is within our reach. Surrendering to God, with the
willingness to obey whatever He says, is the key.

The Spirit longs to introduce us to such reasonings. We understand them through the mind of Christ that we've inherited. I receive
revelation from the Spirit, often with such depth that it is difficult to
fully comprehend it, but I am willing to live with that mystery. (Please
note that such revelation is not *in place of* the revelation of Scripture.)
In fact, a willingness to trust God with what I don't understand often
precedes increased understanding.

Some people say, "We don't need God to speak to us because we have the Bible." This is one of the more popular excuses people use to avoid learning to hear the voice of God. But, in Christ, we have been given the spiritual capacity to hear God's voice. Jesus Himself said, *"My sheep hear My voice"* (John 10:27 NKJV, NASB). The ability to hear Him comes in our *yes* to follow Him. Many believers avoid His voice because, in ignorance, they fear what they can't explain. These believers quarantine themselves from other parts of the body of Christ that have something to offer them to make their lives better: revelation about the Holy Spirit and the way He works. All of us are to be strengthened by what each member of the body provides. It is for the purpose of helping us in our daily life of walking with, and depending on, the Holy Spirit.

Hearing from the Holy Spirit actually drives me *to* the Scriptures. Not only does reading the Scriptures help me to verify whether what I have sensed is biblically correct, but the Spirit's voice also endears me to the Word of God, which brings life with every page. My Bible is Jesus in print. He is the Word of God. The promises, the warnings, the mysteries—all of it represents Him. To love Him but not love His Word is a contradiction. It's my relationship with the Spirit of Christ that draws me into the Word of God over and over again. The time I spend reading and studying Scripture is part of my journey with the Holy Spirit.

Overflow: The Holy Spirit's reasoning is of another world, one much superior to ours in every way.

Reading: Matthew 8:5–13

Reflection: In what ways is the time you spend reading and studying Scripture a part of your journey with the Holy Spirit?

_____

_____

_____

_____

_____

_____

_____

_____

_____

_____

_____

_____

_____

_____

_____

_____

_____

_____

DAY 31

THE HELPER COMPLETES AND EMPOWERS US

"Our soul waits for the LORD; He is our help and our shield."
—Psalm 33:20 (NKJV, NASB)

Today, we will explore further what it means that the Holy Spirit, as our Helper, completes what is lacking in us and how He empowers us. In Genesis 2:18, when God said He was going to give Adam a wife, He described her using the word *"helper."* The expression that has often been used in the church for Eve's role is *helpmate.* Through the years, I've heard many teachings and comments on this word, but while these explanations may have been well-intentioned, they missed the mark miserably.

Historically, the word *helpmate* has been used to describe the "subservient" role of a wife to her husband. Such a poor translation of the word has only added fuel to the ignorance involved in not allowing women to minister. Eve was not less than Adam, and there wasn't competition between them. Eve was both equal to Adam and complementary to him. Likewise, women are not in a subservient role to men, to be controlled or directed, as though they lack the spirituality to discern for themselves.

Even the concept of *submission*, which has been misinterpreted in our times and applied to women in a similar way, is heaven's plan to give us access to multiplied personal and corporate strength. (See, for example, Ephesians 5:18–21.) A married woman is a helpmate to her husband (not the entire human race of males) in the same way that God is a Helper to His people. In the Old Testament, God is called the "helpmate" of Israel thirteen times. (See, for example, Deuteronomy 33:29; Psalm 33:20.) In being Israel's helpmate, He didn't abdicate the throne to become less than a human. Combining the Hebrew words for *"helper suitable"* (Genesis 2:18 NASB), this beautiful phrase basically means "one enabled to stand face-to-face with another, making up all that may be lacking."[6] We understand this idea as it pertains to our relationship with God. He makes up for what is lacking in us. So true. But it is also true in marital relationships that each spouse helps to make up for what is lacking in the other.

The tangible illustration of the relationship between a husband and wife given to us in Scripture is ultimately a picture of the Holy Spirit—the promised One Jesus called "Helper"—and His relationship to God's people. He is the One who stands face-to-face with us, ensuring that we come into the fullness of all that God intended.

When the Hebrew word rendered as *"helper"* in Genesis 2:18 is used in relation to God in other places in the Old Testament, it normally pertains to His sending military might to assist His people in a crisis. As our Helper, God fights on behalf of His people. The Holy Spirit uses all the tools in His arsenal to draw us to the Father and conform us to the image of His Son, Jesus Christ.

⌒

Overflow: The Holy Spirit is the One who stands face-to-face with us, ensuring that we come into the fullness of all that God intended.

Reading: Psalm 33:13–22

---

6. "Genesis 2:18," NASB Lexicon, Bible Hub, https://biblehub.com/lexicon/genesis/2-18.htm; Jeff A. Benner, "What Is a Help Meet?" Ancient Hebrew Research Center, https://www.ancient-hebrew.org/studies-interpretation/what-is-a-help-meet.htm.

Reflection: In what ways have you recently experienced God as your Helper?

_____

_____

_____

_____

_____

_____

_____

_____

_____

_____

_____

_____

_____

_____

_____

_____

_____

_____

_____

_____

DAY 32

THE HELPER LEADS US IN KINGDOM PRAYING

"Your kingdom come.
Your will be done on earth as it is in heaven."
—Luke 11:2 (NKJV)

I'm sure that if Jesus were sitting right in front of you, you—like me—would want Him to teach you many things, because this world has never seen a teacher like Him. His perception of the Father and His heart impact me deeply. Most of us could probably write a book of questions we'd like to have answered and knowledge we'd love to learn from the greatest Teacher who ever lived. And yet those who were always with Him, who were the most acquainted with His life and ministry, only asked to be taught one thing: how to pray. Understanding what Jesus taught about prayer will help us to align our prayers with God's will and the leading of the Holy Spirit.

Now it came to pass, as He was praying in a certain place, when He ceased, that one of His disciples said to Him, "Lord, teach us to pray, as John also taught his disciples." So He said to them, "When you pray, say: 'Our Father in heaven, hallowed be Your name. Your kingdom come. Your will be done on earth as it is in heaven. Give us day by day our daily bread. And forgive us our sins, for we also forgive everyone who is indebted to us. And do not lead us into temptation, but deliver us from the evil one.'"

(Luke 11:1–4 NKJV)

Jesus's response to this request was to teach His followers "the Disciples' Prayer" (this seems a more appropriate title to me than "the Lord's Prayer" since it is a model for us). I don't think Jesus said this prayer over and over again when He prayed all night on the mountain. (See, for example, Luke 6:12–16.) Neither do I think He was giving His disciples a prayer that would limit their hearts' expression to the Father, thus creating a religious routine. I actually love praying this prayer in Matthew's version. (See Matthew 6:9–13.) But in my way of thinking, this model prayer was given to us to highlight appropriate priorities we need to keep in mind whenever we approach the Father. More specifically, we see the following priorities in the prayer Jesus taught: worshipping the Father, praying for heaven's reality to invade earth now, acknowledging the need for provision, embracing a commitment to live a lifestyle of forgiveness, and realizing we are in a spiritual battle and thus asking for protection.

These are highlights of intentional prayer. They represent the basic needs of every believer. We are to use them as a guide as we allow the Holy Spirit to lead us in our prayers. But while following this focus in our prayers is important and effective, there is so much more that we need to know and do, and this again is where our Helper makes up for what we lack.

Overflow: Understanding what Jesus taught about prayer will help us to align our prayers with God's will and the leading of the Holy Spirit.

Reading: Matthew 6:5–13

Reflection: In your own words, how would you phrase the priorities of the kingdom of God that Jesus taught in His model prayer? Which priorities are you currently emphasizing in your prayers? Which do you need to incorporate?

_____

_____

_____

_____

_____

_____

_____

_____

_____

_____

_____

_____

_____

_____

_____

_____

_____

_____

_____

DAY 33

THE HELPER INTERCEDES FOR US

"The Spirit...makes intercession for the saints
according to the will of God."
—Romans 8:27 (NKJV)

As our Helper, the Holy Spirit also prays on our behalf. The apostle Paul addresses the issue of effective prayer in Romans 8, which, to me, is one of the most fulfilling and inviting chapters in the whole Bible. There is so much to glean from this chapter, especially as it pertains to the person of the Holy Spirit. But here's the passage I want us to look at:

> *Likewise the Spirit also helps in our weaknesses. For we do not know what we should pray for as we ought, but the Spirit Himself makes intercession for us with groanings which cannot be uttered. Now He who searches the hearts knows what the mind of the Spirit is, because He makes intercession for the saints according to the will of God.... Christ who died, and furthermore is also risen,...is even at the right hand of God, who also makes intercession for us.* (Romans 8:26–27, 34 NKJV)

This is a remarkable passage. Paul acknowledges that we don't know what we're doing when we pray. Knowing our priorities in prayer isn't enough. It is almost as if Jesus, in wanting to fully answer the one request of His own disciples to teach them to pray, gave the

Holy Spirit to believers as the Teacher of prayer and worship. We know that one of the main influences of the Spirit of God is that of a teacher. And when we speak in tongues—in an unknown language enabled by the Holy Spirit—the tongues can be either prayer or worship.

We see this combination reflected in Romans 8. While I don't necessarily believe that the *"groanings"* of the Spirit that Paul speaks about in this passage are the same as praying in tongues, I do think they are a description of the Holy Spirit praying through a surrendered believer. In Galatians, Paul makes an extreme statement that I believe refers to intercessory prayer: *"My children, with whom I am again in labor until Christ is formed in you"* (Galatians 4:19 NASB). The *"labor"* spoken of in this verse is a picture of deep prayer. It involves groanings—beyond words.

I can't pretend to understand all of this, but I can delight in it. Consider how remarkable it is that both the Holy Spirit and Jesus pray. And They pray for us!

Now look at the verse that is sandwiched in between the ones describing the two great Intercessors, Jesus and the Holy Spirit: *"And we know that all things work together for good to those who love God, to those who are the called according to His purpose"* (Romans 8:28 NKJV). No wonder *"all things work together for good."* Our legal Advocate and our Redeemer both appear before the Father, pleading our case!

Overflow: Consider how remarkable it is that both the Holy Spirit and Jesus pray. And They pray for us!

Reading: Romans 8:26–39

Reflection: Will you surrender today, and each day, to the Holy Spirit, asking Him to pray through you for the will of God to be done on earth as it is in heaven?

_____

_____

_____

_____

_____

_____

_____

_____

_____

_____

_____

_____

_____

_____

_____

_____

_____

_____

DAY 34

GOD SPEAKS BOTH SUBTLY AND AUDIBLY

"Speak, LORD, for Your servant is listening."
—1 Samuel 3:9 (NASB, NIV)

God speaks to us in various ways, among them subtle ideas to our minds and either loud or soft communications. The voice of the Lord is often an internal, familiar voice that introduces a thought or insight we had not previously considered. What comes to us is usually not something we would have thought of on our own. Yet people often take credit for the thoughts they receive in such moments, believing they just accidentally stumbled on an idea. I don't think this mistake comes from arrogance as much as from ignorance. They just don't understand how subtle God's voice can be. He speaks to our inner man, interweaving His mind into our experiences, surroundings, and feelings in a most mysterious way.

Often, someone will say, "I can't hear God's voice, but I do feel His peace." They rarely seem to realize that the peace they feel *is* His voice. Since He is the Word of God, His presence is a manifestation of His voice. That concept just hasn't reached our minds yet. My personal conviction is that He often deposits insights into our spirit-man that are to be brought out in the coming hours or days. We must learn to always stay tender to God—not just when there's a crisis or an urgent need.

God may also sometimes speak to us audibly. This form of communication is much less common, but it does occur. I've heard the audible voice of God twice. It is unmistakable and impossible to miss, although we may need to discern what we are hearing. A biblical example of this is when God spoke to the prophet Samuel when he was just a boy serving under Eli the priest:

> *Samuel was lying down in the temple of the LORD where the ark of God was, that the LORD called Samuel; and he said, "Here I am." Then he ran to Eli and said, "Here I am, for you called me." But he said, "I did not call, lie down again." So he went and lay down. The LORD called yet again, "Samuel!" So Samuel arose and went to Eli and said, "Here I am, for you called me." But he answered, "I did not call, my son, lie down again." Now Samuel did not yet know the LORD, nor had the word of the LORD yet been revealed to him. So the LORD called Samuel again for the third time. And he arose and went to Eli and said, "Here I am, for you called me." Then Eli discerned that the LORD was calling the boy. And Eli said to Samuel, "Go lie down, and it shall be if He calls you, that you shall say, 'Speak, LORD, for Your servant is listening.'"* (1 Samuel 3:1–9 NASB)

Overflow: God speaks to our inner man, interweaving His mind into our experiences, surroundings, and feelings in a most mysterious way.

Reading: 1 Kings 19:9–18

Reflection: How often do you pray, "Speak, Lord, for Your servant is listening"? How might you be more attentive to the Lord's voice in your day-to-day life?

_____

_____

_____

_____

_____

_____

_____

_____

_____

_____

_____

_____

_____

_____

_____

_____

_____

DAY 35

THE LORD SPEAKS DURING WORSHIP

"While they were worshiping the Lord and fasting, the Holy Spirit said, 'Set apart for me Barnabas and Saul for the work to which I have called them.'"
—Acts 13:2 (NIV)

In addition to hearing from God either through subtle ideas or audibly, we can hear from Him as we draw near to Him in worship, where He will deposit the specifics of His Word deeply into our hearts. He will then bring these truths to the surface at the moment they are most needed. The Holy Spirit is the great worship leader in heaven, as all worship is in spirit. (See John 4:24.) Worship is a Holy Spirit activity. As such, it is one of the most practical ways to learn to recognize God's presence and, in doing so, learn His heart and mind. The affectionate expression of worship is a way of demonstrating our surrender to God while encountering Him.

The bliss, the perfect pleasure and union, between worshippers and God might best be represented by the meaning of one of the Greek words for *worship* used in the New Testament: "to kiss towards."[7] It implies an affectionate response to God. We have the distinct privilege of ministering to God directly. A priest, the position to which all New Testament believers are called (see, for example, Revelation 1:5–6), is one who ministers directly to the Lord. I

---

7. *Strong's*, G4352, Blue Letter Bible Lexicon, https://www.blueletterbible.org/lexicon/g4352/kjv/tr/0-1/.

believe that, for this reason, many songs have been written in the last thirty years or so that speak directly *to* God, not just *about* Him, or even about important concepts in theology, although both of those aspects are important as well. Ministering to God implies a one-on-one relationship, even when we are in a crowd.

Thus, sometimes we hear the voice of the Lord through inspired thoughts, ideas, or impressions, whether during the course of our everyday lives or in our times of prayer or worship. This may not be as direct a means of communication as we might wish for. Yet God has access to everything in our present, past, and future, and He will use all of it to bring about His purposes in us.

When people realize that what they thought was their idea actually came from God, it strengthens their faith immensely. Knowing you hear from God is more encouraging and rewarding than thinking everything comes to you because you are a genius with creative ideas. Even where true natural genius is involved, so is God. It's much more gratifying to see how we fit into the bigger picture of co-laboring with God than it is to fulfill the demands of our ego. Knowing we've heard the voice of God is both humbling and exalting at the same time. It's another one of those apparent contradictions, or paradoxes, that exist only in the kingdom of God.

God speaks in countless other ways. But the three we have reviewed in the last two devotions—hearing from God subtly, hearing from Him audibly, and receiving from Him through worship—are enough for now as we continue on our relational journey with the Holy Spirit.

Overflow: The affectionate expression of worship is a way of demonstrating our surrender to God while encountering Him.

Reading: Acts 13

Reflection: What does it mean to you that you are called to be a priest to the Lord, ministering directly to Him? How do you fulfill this role in your worship of God?

_____

_____

_____

_____

_____

_____

_____

_____

_____

_____

_____

_____

_____

_____

_____

_____

_____

_____

DAY 36

PREPARING OUR HEARTS, PART 1: SEEK WHAT GOD HAS HIDDEN AND ANTICIPATE HIS VOICE

*"It is the glory of God to conceal a matter,
but the glory of kings is to search out a matter."*
—Proverbs 25:2 (NKJV, NASB)

I think each of us wishes we heard from God better than we do. Several times, I've noticed that when someone says they want to hear God's voice better, another person will respond, "Stop looking up. Just look down at your Bible. He spoke through Scripture." And while I think this is a cute response, as the Scriptures are the basis for our hearing from God, it does little to answer the cry of the heart for a relationship of interaction with a Father who loves us dearly. It is in our DNA to long to hear His voice in a personal way. Our life in Christ started because He individually called us to Himself, and we responded to that call.

How do we prepare our hearts to hear what God is saying to us through the Holy Spirit? The first way is to actively seek what He has hidden for us and desires to share with us. *"It is the glory of God to conceal a matter, but the glory of kings is to search out a matter."* Solomon made this declaration in Proverbs 25:2 (NKJV, NASB). The beautiful part of this reality is discovering that God hides things *for* us, not *from* us. They are there to be searched for. The second part of the verse says that it's the glory of kings *"to search out a matter."* In other words, our royalty in Christ is never more clearly pronounced than when we live with the realization that the mysteries of God's kingdom are there for our discovery. Perhaps we could state it in this way: the muscle of royalty is developed through its use in pursuing the mysteries of God. It's the adventurous heart of a child that best represents the kingly in God's kingdom. Children are always in pursuit of more. *"Do not fear, little flock, for it is your Father's good pleasure to give you the kingdom"* (Luke 12:32 NKJV).

Another way we can prepare our hearts to hear what God is saying to us through the Holy Spirit is to actively anticipate hearing His still, small voice. (See 1 Kings 19:12 NKJV.) Learning to "lean in," or pay close attention, helps. I've heard the still, small voice of God countless times. And I am certain I have missed it many times— sometimes out of my resolve to do my own will, and sometimes because of anxiety or fear that dominated the moment. Often, God's voice has to be anticipated in order to be heard. It's so easy to miss it or talk yourself out of the impression you have just received from God. Since words become presence, recognizing a word from God will assist you in discerning when He is at work. Jesus said it this way: "My words to you are Spirit, and they are life." (See John 6:63.) Words from the Spirit manifest God's presence, and His presence gives life. That is the economy of God's heart and mind. It is manifest more often than we think.

⌐‿‿‿¬

Overflow: It's the adventurous heart of a child that best represents the kingly in God's kingdom.

Reading: Matthew 7:7–11

Reflection: How often do you anticipate hearing God's voice as you worship, pray, and look to Him for guidance? How might you increase that anticipation?

_____

_____

_____

_____

_____

_____

_____

_____

_____

_____

_____

_____

_____

_____

_____

_____

DAY 37

PREPARING OUR HEARTS, PART 2: REMEMBER WHAT GOD HAS ALREADY SPOKEN

"Mary treasured all these things, pondering them in her heart."
—Luke 2:19 (NASB)

One of the ways people often punish someone else is by refusing to speak to or acknowledge the other person. We call this behavior "giving the silent treatment." God is often silent toward us in the sense that He does not use obvious, overt ways of speaking and communicating, but that does not mean He is giving us the silent treatment as a punishment. His silence takes some getting used to, especially when our level of hunger for Him has increased dramatically. God is often silent because He has already spoken to us (perhaps in the subtle way of the still, small voice), and it's up to us to remember/recall/discover what He has said in a previous season of our lives. Often, we face challenges that He has prepared us for, but we don't feel ready because we haven't held on with faith to the things He has previously spoken.

Mary the mother of Jesus is my favorite example of someone who exercised the discipline of both hearing and remembering:

At Jesus's birth, after hearing the shepherds describe how the angels appeared to them and what they said about Jesus, *"Mary treasured all these things, pondering them in her heart"* (Luke 2:19 NASB).

After Mary and Joseph searched for Jesus for three days and found Him in the temple, talking with the religious leaders, "[Jesus] *went down with them* [Mary and Joseph] *and came to Nazareth, and He continued in subjection to them; and His mother treasured all these things in her heart*" (Luke 2:51 NASB).

Mary treasured God's words to her, including those spoken to her by Jesus. She "pondered them in her heart," which implies she mulled over them in her heart and mind, day after day. As the mystery of the life of Jesus unfolded, Mary no doubt recognized that it was the Lord who had prepared her for the events Jesus was about to experience through the word of the Lord. It implies that she highly valued the words she had been given and did not consider them a random addition to her life; in fact, they gave her a central focus for why she was alive: to manifest Jesus to the world.

When Mary treasured the words of the Lord concerning her life and, ultimately, the life of her Son, she esteemed them too much to abuse them through improper use. I doubt very much that she fully understood what the angel was saying to her when he announced that she would conceive the Messiah by the Holy Spirit. Again, this is often one of the ways we know God has spoken to us: He speaks outside of what we would reason or plan for ourselves. Plus, He often speaks to us in a way that invites us to seek Him more, as well as to depend upon Him for understanding—both for the word itself and for seeing that word fulfilled.

Overflow: One of the ways we know God has spoken to us is that He speaks outside of what we would reason or plan for ourselves.

Reading: Luke 2:8–19

Reflection: What might you need to remember or discover about what God has already spoken to you? How will you respond to God's promises and instructions?

_____

_____

_____

_____

_____

_____

_____

_____

_____

_____

_____

_____

_____

_____

_____

_____

_____

_____

_____

DAY 38

PREPARING OUR HEARTS, PART 3: ALLOW YOUR HEART TO REST IN GOD

*"Come to Me, all who are weary and heavy-laden,
and I will give you rest."*
—Matthew 11:28 (NASB)

We hear best when our hearts are at rest. But, honestly, my need to hear from God is at its highest level when I am anxious and afraid. Hearing is what brings me to a place of trust and rest. It's what reintroduces me to peace. Therefore, the painful reality is that when I most need a word from God, I'm most likely to miss it due to my anxiety. Thankfully, being aware of this conflict helps because the fix is simple. I didn't say it is *easy*, but it is simple, like most kingdom solutions: acknowledging God's lordship. Our acknowledgment of His lordship fixes most problems.

Feeling bad about our anxious feelings doesn't bring us rest. And mere acknowledgment of wrong thinking doesn't create right thinking. But true repentance does. Repentance is illustrated in two words: *from* and *toward*, as in *"repentance **from** dead works and...faith **toward** God"* (Hebrews 6:1 NKJV, NASB). Again, regretting my anxiety doesn't remove it, but dealing with the cause does. At the root of anxiety and fear is misplaced trust. We need to repent for trusting in anything other than God, whether it is our opinions, resources, experiences, or the ideals, thoughts, and values of others. They all compete for that one place that only God deserves—our God, in whom we trust. Only One is perfectly faithful. Not to trust Him is the essence of foolishness.

Sometimes we miss our opportunity to repent because, as I mentioned above, we think a simple acknowledgment of our error fixes everything. It doesn't. It is godly sorrow that leads us to repentance. (See 2 Corinthians 7:10.) Too many people have sorrow for the pain that their sin has caused in their lives, but not sorrow for the sin itself. The pain of realizing how we've hurt the heart of our Father is the kind of pain that leads us to abandon the sin altogether.

Thus, whenever we find ourselves filled with anxiety or fear and unable to hear God's voice, we have several tools to help us begin hearing again. The first is to quiet our hearts into a place of rest and trust in God's sovereignty in our lives. As we confess our lack of trust, we should also confess all known sin, as this is an obvious place to restore our relationship with God. Confession draws the great Forgiver into our situation. We should also worship the Lord, because worship is an intimate expression of affection and adoration toward God. Another tool is to meditate on God's Word. His Word reveals His mind. Whenever we meditate on the Word, the Author shows up, helping to establish His heart in ours. Additionally, it is critical for us to learn to confess and declare all that God has promised us in His Word. Aligning our response to our situations with His mind and thoughts will bring breakthrough, often enabling us to play a responsible part in seeing the fulfillment of His promises.

Overflow: We need to repent for trusting in anything other than God, whether it is our opinions, resources, experiences, or the ideals, thoughts, and values of others.

Reading: Matthew 11:28–30

Reflection: Are anxiety and worry blocking you from hearing from God in a particular situation? Set aside time to consider how your emotions may be affecting your spiritual hearing and to offer God true repentance for any lack of trust in His lordship and faithfulness. Then, allow your heart to trust in Him fully.

_____

_____

_____

_____

_____

_____

_____

_____

_____

_____

_____

_____

_____

_____

_____

_____

DAY 39

PREPARING OUR HEARTS, PART 4: RECEIVE GOD'S WORD EVEN WHEN IT IS PERPLEXING

"Lord, to whom shall we go? You have words of eternal life."
—John 6:68 (NASB)

We must understand that there is the overt voice of God and there is the covert voice of God. The overt voice of God is specific to a need or question. It is much more obvious and outward, and it is not very easy to miss if you're looking and listening for it. The covert voice of God is manifested in His presence rather than in concepts or specifics. When we understand this, we learn how to maintain abiding faith when things don't seem to make sense or give us the clarity we are crying out for. Recognizing the difference between these two aspects of God's voice is critical to helping us grow in challenging times.

For me, one of the most fascinating stories in the entire Bible is the account in John 6 of the multiplication of the loaves and fish, as well as what occurred afterward. The crowd that had gathered to hear Jesus that day was massive, so thousands upon thousands of people were present to partake of this provision. Yet the crowds were gathered not only to see Jesus's miracles but also to hear Him speak, because no one had ever spoken the way He did. Over and over again, whenever He spoke, the crowds were stunned at His teaching.

But the following day, most people's attitude toward Jesus and His teaching shifted. Jesus began to explain that the only way to be one of His disciples was to "eat His flesh and drink His blood." As you read through John 6, you note the outrage from the crowd when they hear Jesus's words. The Twelve no doubt wanted Jesus to offer an explanation, as they likely loved Jesus's (and their) newfound popularity with the people. But now they saw the crowds leaving in disgust. The Scriptures even record that some of His most committed followers left that day. (See verse 66.) They couldn't handle the conflict of ideas in their minds, the God-given mystery.

Once more, it's apparent that all of us need to face the tension found in mystery. Even Jesus's proven disciples needed this challenge. God is a Father who rewards those who seek Him. And there are no rewards where there are no choices to be made. Jesus already knew who wouldn't respond well to this challenge and who would respond well (responding to mystery with abiding faith). He knew who would not believe and who would believe. Faith is the intended outcome of His voice. Always. *"Faith comes by hearing"* (Romans 10:17 NKJV). Jesus is trustworthy, a truth we proclaim in every act of faith toward Him—even abiding faith in the midst of mystery.

Overflow: The covert voice of God is manifested in His presence rather than in concepts or specifics.

Reading: John 6:35–69

Reflection: What words that God has spoken to you, either in Scripture or personally, have perplexed you? How have you responded? How might you deepen your faith response in such times?

_____

_____

_____

_____

_____

_____

_____

_____

_____

_____

_____

_____

_____

_____

_____

_____

DAY 40

ASKING FOR ANYTHING

*"If you abide in Me, and My words abide in you, you will ask
what you desire, and it shall be done for you."*
—John 15:7 (NKJV)

In John 14–16, Jesus unveils the ultimate feature of our design in
God's image in that, with the Holy Spirit living in us, we are posi-
tioned to *ask for anything, and it will be done.* We can pray for all
aspects of God's heavenly kingdom to come to earth and see them
fulfilled through the power of His Spirit. What I find interesting is
that, in those three chapters, where Jesus promises His disciples four
times that their desires will be fulfilled (see John 14:13–14; 15:7, 16;
16:23–24), He also states that the Holy Spirit is called the Helper
and would be given to them by the Father (see John 14:16, 26; 15:26;
16:7). This title for the Spirit is mentioned four times in these three
chapters. I don't think this is a coincidence. Four times, the disciples
are invited to ask for anything, and it would be done. And four times,
the Holy Spirit is described as the Helper.

Dreaming big is supposed to be a result of our yielded relationship with the Holy Spirit and His influence on our future. Jesus is the
One who said, "Abide in Me, and let My words abide in you, and anything you ask for will be done for you." Is it humility for us to pray,
"Not my will, but Yours" (see Luke 22:42) in this situation? Before
you answer, consider again that four times in three chapters, Jesus
tells His disciples that anything they desire will be done for them.

In John 16:24 (NKJV), He says, *"Ask, and you will receive, that your joy may be full."* Receiving answers to our prayers and desires is the key to fullness of joy. The pathway to such significance in prayer is learning to pray the will of God. We become shaped in that process—so much so that He wants to hear our will! It's a scary invitation, for sure. And yet it is part of the mystery and paradox of the gospel life, where we die to live (see, for example, John 12:24–25), and we go low to rise high (see, for example, Luke 14:11).

We know that Jesus didn't promote a self-centered gospel where we use a magic wand to make all our wishes come to pass. That would be the opposite of all He taught and illustrated. And yet by telling His disciples to ask for what they wanted, He drew them into something that was far outside their understanding or experience—something beyond even the point of reference of much of Israel's history. Although God would carry out His purposes in His timing and wisdom, He was still interested in their desires! And this is the essential point we so often miss in our relationship with God.

⌒

Overflow: We become shaped in the process of learning to pray the will of God—so much so that He wants to hear our will!

Reading: John 15:1–17

Reflection: What prayers is the Holy Spirit prompting you to pray as you align your will with God's? How have you been nourishing your faith to pray them?

_____

_____

_____

_____

_____

_____

_____

_____

_____

_____

_____

_____

_____

_____

_____

_____

PART THREE:

OVERFLOWING

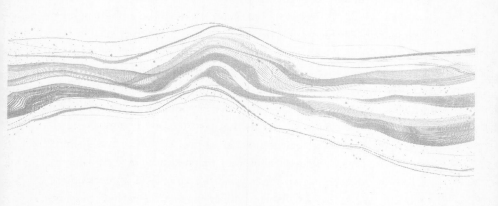

DAY 41

FILLED TO OVERFLOWING

"You have anointed my head with oil; my cup overflows."
—Psalm 23:5 (NASB)

We are surrounded by impossibilities in our world. And yet at the core of the gospel is this declaration: *"Nothing will be impossible with God"* (Luke 1:37 NASB). That's not meant to be a philosophical statement that helps us feel better about the difficulties of life. It is heaven's bold decree that is to have measurable outcomes. It's a declaration that is looking for earthly partners to help bring about *on earth as it is in heaven.* Impossibilities must bend their knee to the name of Jesus flowing from our lips. This must happen, for it is the miracle realm that testifies and proclaims that Jesus is raised from the dead. If there is no resurrection, then we are all wasting our time. If Jesus wasn't raised from the dead, then we won't be raised, either. There is no heaven, no eternity, no life beyond our time here on earth. (See 1 Corinthians 15:14–20.) Without the resurrection, we have permission to live for ourselves. Yet if Jesus was raised from the dead, then nothing matters more—and He was raised!

Being baptized in the Holy Spirit immerses us in the same Spirit who raised Jesus from the dead—the Spirit of resurrection. In fact, we are born again because the resurrection Spirit of Christ comes to dwell in us. His resurrection life becomes our new life. The life of power is the normal Christian life, and it started with the defeat of sin, death, the powers of darkness, and the grave. Jesus pushed this issue beyond what anyone would have asked for or expected, saying that those who believe in Him would do *"greater works"* than He did. (See John 14:12.) And the *"works"* spoken of in that passage refer, without question, to the miracle realm.

Often, when I teach people about this subject of being filled with the Spirit, I hold an unopened water bottle before them and then ask if the water bottle is full. Of course, it is full for the purpose of the sale. But the height of the water is clearly an inch or so below the top of the bottle. So, technically, the bottle isn't completely full. Then I take another bottle of water and slowly begin to pour its contents into the bottle I just opened, asking people to tell me when it's full. It quickly becomes obvious that the bottle really is full only when it begins to overflow. In the same way that abundance in the kingdom is not measured by what we contain but by what we have given away, so it is with the fullness of the Spirit: we are filled with the Spirit only when there is overflow.

Overflow: Abundance in the kingdom is not measured by what we contain but by what we have given away.

Reading: Matthew 10:1–8

Reflection: How are you partnering with God to help bring about *on earth as it is in heaven?*

DAY 42

DOING THE IMPOSSIBLE

"And lo, I am with you always, even to the end of the age."
—Matthew 28:20 (NASB)

As we receive God's Spirit (hosting His indwelling) and remain submitted to Him (allowing Him to rest upon us), He will use us to carry out His purposes for the world. We saw earlier that the Scriptures specifically say God was with Jesus as He went about His ministry, doing miraculous works of healing and deliverance. And one of the most fascinating things I have found in my study of both the Old and New Testament is the fact that when God tells a person, "I will be with you," that message is almost always connected to an impossible assignment for that individual.

Likewise, when Jesus appeared to the eleven remaining disciples after His death and resurrection and commissioned them into their reason for being, He told them He would be with them:

> Go therefore and make disciples of all the nations, baptizing them in the name of the Father and the Son and the Holy Spirit, teaching them to observe all that I commanded you; ***and lo, I am with you always***, even to the end of the age.
>
> (Matthew 28:19–20 NASB)

Those first disciples—and all future disciples—were given an assignment: *"make disciples of all the nations."* This may be the most overwhelming assignment ever given to anyone. All of us as believers inherit this commission. But the one thing that makes this assignment doable is the fact that *God is with us.* At this point, it is vital for us to remember that God enables what He commands.

Hopefully, by now, the point is obvious: when God is revealed to be with someone, it is because He expects something impossible to be done. It's the nature of our Father. The gospel invites us to function beyond human ability through the power of the Holy Spirit. And it's the Father who ensures that His requirement of invading the impossible is possible. *"With men this is impossible, but with God all things are possible"* (Matthew 19:26 NKJV). It's as though, when God is revealed to be with someone, all of heaven lines up to see what we will conquer in His name.

It was the presence of the Holy Spirit upon Jesus that made the miraculous not only possible but logical. It was to be expected that the impossibilities of life would bow before the Spirit of God that rested on the Son of God. The light of God's power is infinite. Darkness, along with its manifestations of affliction and torment, is finite. Wherever the Holy Spirit demonstrates the absolute majesty of Jesus, victory and liberty are the outcome.

We know that we can do nothing without Jesus. The great tragedy is that we've learned to do nothing *with* Him. But that paradox is changing in this hour, as God is making His "presence assignment" clearly known. It is time for the Father to be revealed through a group of yielded believers whose dreams take them into the impossible for the glory of God.

Overflow: God enables what He commands.

Reading: Exodus 3:1–12

Reflection: What "impossible" assignment has God called you to do in His strength? How have you responded to that call?

_____

_____

_____

_____

_____

_____

_____

_____

_____

_____

_____

_____

_____

_____

_____

_____

_____

_____

DAY 43

THE RIVER FLOWED THROUGH JESUS

*"He cast out the spirits with a word,
and healed all who were sick."*
—Matthew 8:16 (NKJV)

Even in His earthly ministry, Jesus modeled the victorious life that would be common after His resurrection. He healed the sick before making the payment for their healing by the stripes He bore, mentioned in Isaiah 53:

> *Surely He has borne our griefs and carried our sorrows…. But He was wounded for our transgressions, He was bruised for our iniquities; the chastisement for our peace was upon Him, and by His stripes we were healed.* (Isaiah 53:4–5 NKJV)

The Hebrew words translated *"griefs"* and *"sorrows"* are literally "sicknesses" and "pains," respectively.[8] In fact, when Jesus quoted this passage in Matthew 8:17 (NKJV), He actually used the words *"infirmities"* and *"sicknesses."*[9] The prophet Isaiah declared there would be a transaction that would make healing available and free. All of the healings and miracles that Jesus performed occurred before His sufferings. It reminds me of when my wife and I would take our children

---

8. "Isaiah 53:4," NASB Lexicon, Bible Hub, https://biblehub.com/lexicon/isaiah/53-4.htm.
9. *NKJV Spirit-Filled Life Bible*, 1032.

with us when we went grocery shopping. They would be in the cart as we piled in the groceries. But we would often go down the ice cream aisle first, grab ice cream bars for them, and let them eat the ice cream while we shopped. It kept them happy, which in turn kept us happy. In reality, they were eating something that wasn't paid for. We would simply put the wrappers in the cart and pay for the ice cream before we left the store. What Jesus did is similar. Everyone He ministered to was healed, and He paid for their healings before leaving "the store" (this earthly realm).

The woman with the issue of blood had borne that affliction in her body for many years. No physician could help her. But then she heard about Jesus, who knew no impossibility. While everyone was pressing in close and touching Jesus, she alone saw what was available to her in that touch. Her perception gave her access to the miracle. As soon as she accessed it, Jesus stopped and said that someone had touched Him. The crowd, including the disciples, couldn't understand why He would make such a statement because the most obvious thing in that moment was the crowd pressing in to be close to Jesus. And yet Jesus recognized power flowing from Him. That's the river. That's the Spirit of the living God that flowed from Him. And the woman was healed.

Jesus recognized the presence of God flowing from Him, which tells me He lived with a consciousness of the indwelling Holy Spirit. Developing an awareness of Him is one of our greatest privileges and responsibilities. Again, the normal Christian life is a life where the River flows from us.

⌒

Overflow: Jesus modeled the victorious life that would be common after His resurrection.

Reading: Luke 8:43–48

Reflection: Do you have an increasing awareness of the indwelling Holy Spirit in your life? How might you further develop that awareness?

_____

_____

_____

_____

_____

_____

_____

_____

_____

_____

_____

_____

_____

_____

_____

_____

_____

DAY 44

THE RIVER FLOWED THROUGH
THE APOSTLES

"Freely you have received, freely give."
—Matthew 10:8

The river that flowed through Jesus was meant to flow through those who follow Him. The disciples, turned apostles, were the first to experience this wonder. I'm still amazed at Peter's confidence in what he carried. When he spoke to a man who had been lame since birth, he knew he possessed the miracle power of God that was within him and was about to flow through him:

> Then Peter said, *"Silver and gold I do not have, but **what I do have I give you:** In the name of Jesus Christ of Nazareth, rise up and walk."* And he took him by the right hand and lifted him up, and **immediately his feet and ankle bones received strength.** *So he, leaping up, stood and walked and entered the temple with them—walking, leaping, and praising God.* (Acts 3:6–8 NKJV)

Notice that the release of God's presence, the release of the miracle, was declared or commanded. Peter said, *"In the name of Jesus Christ of Nazareth, rise up and walk."* The miracle was voice-activated. The disciples were trained in this way of thinking early in their journey with Jesus. It was the model He gave them for all ministry:

*And as you go, preach, saying, "The kingdom of heaven is at hand." Heal the sick, cleanse the lepers, raise the dead, cast out demons. **Freely you have received, freely give.***

(Matthew 10:7–8 NKJV)

"Freely you have received, freely give." What have you received? *Him.* The Holy Spirit.

[Jesus said,] *"Most assuredly, I say to you, he who believes in Me, the works that I do he will do also; and greater works than these he will do, because I go to My Father. And whatever you ask in My name, that I will do, that the Father may be glorified in the Son. If you ask anything in My name, I will do it."*

(John 14:12–14 NKJV)

As we cooperate with the Spirit, He can flow from us freely, impacting every room we enter, every situation we give our attention to. This is the character of the life of someone filled with the Holy Spirit. This is the life of ministry, for in ministry we are actually releasing the presence of God into broken situations.

One of the ways I describe it is like this: The Holy Spirit is in you—and He wants out! He is in us as a river, not a lake. Rivers flow and alter the geography around them. It's not that He flows from us and is no longer with us. That's impossible because Jesus promised never to leave us. (See John 14:16–18.) Jesus is eternal and unlimited. The Scriptures say of Him that He had the Spirit without measure. (See John 3:34.) It's the same for each of us who have received the gift of the indwelling Holy Spirit.

~

Overflow: In ministry we are actually releasing the presence of God into broken situations.

Reading: Matthew 10:1–8

Reflection: In what ways is the river of the Holy Spirit flowing through you to release the presence of God into broken situations? How are you cooperating with the Spirit in this process?

_____

_____

_____

_____

_____

_____

_____

_____

_____

_____

_____

_____

_____

_____

_____

_____

_____

_____

DAY 45

LIVING IN THE FLOW OF THE SPIRIT

"So he, leaping up, stood and walked and entered the temple
with them—walking, leaping, and praising God."
—Acts 3:8 (NKJV)

I've often heard wonderful men and women of God talk about the flow of the Holy Spirit. It's a brilliant way to describe their experience of the River that is in them. Learning to recognize and cooperate with Him is one of the great highlights or privileges in life. We fall into error and make mistakes when we think we can control or direct His activities. The Spirit will not be controlled by us. Yet, as I have expressed, an equally disturbing failure is to pull ourselves out of a position to be used by God to help bring about the desires of His heart: miracles, signs, and wonders. To disqualify ourselves from what He has qualified us for is one of the ultimate expressions of self-will and arrogance.

Spiritual breakthroughs happen through those who obey God's voice. And those who hear His voice well enough to obey it are usually those who believe these breakthroughs are His desire in the first place and seek His face to bring them about. They are usually willing to take whatever risk is necessary to see God's will manifested on earth as it is in heaven. To put it another way: merely a willingness to hear and obey God's command is often not enough. That puts the responsibility entirely on God's shoulders to do something He has already revealed in the Scriptures as being His will. In my experience, being able to hear His command is often the result of seeking His face for a greater measure of breakthrough. It's often far more than seeking God for a specific situation, although that would certainly be appropriate. It is usually the result of seeking God for a greater demonstration of who He is, what He is like, and what He wills through the life of the one seeking His face.

Peter's experience with the man who was lame from birth was noteworthy. As he and John were walking to the temple to pray, they saw this man asking for money. Peter told him to look at them, and then fixed his gaze upon him. *"Peter said, 'Silver and gold I do not have, but what I do have I give you: In the name of Jesus Christ of Nazareth, rise up and walk'"* (Acts 3:6 NKJV).

Peter didn't have what the man was asking for. But he did have what the man needed and certainly would have asked for if he thought it was available or possible: healing. As a result of Peter's releasing what he possessed—the presence of the Holy Spirit—the lame man walked.

How do you allow the Holy Spirit to flow from you? Move in faith as best you know how, and do so from a place of compassion. Faith and compassion come from the Holy Spirit, so living with an awareness of Him positions us for the victories we long for. This will create a lifestyle in which, more and more, you will see that He flows from you to others.

Overflow: Spiritual breakthroughs happen through those who obey God's voice.

Reading: Acts 3:1–10

Reflection: Have you knowingly or unknowingly disqualified yourself from the miracles, signs, and wonders for which God has qualified you through His Spirit and for His glory? If so, how will you begin to change your mindset about this beginning today? How does the example of Peter and John and the lame man encourage you?

_____

_____

_____

_____

_____

_____

_____

_____

_____

_____

_____

_____

_____

_____

_____

_____

DAY 46

RELEASING GOD'S PRESENCE, PART 1: THE SPOKEN WORD

"Just say the word, and my servant will be healed."
—Matthew 8:8 (NASB)

The following passage speaks of the effect of the river that brings life to everything it touches, including nations (see Revelation 22:2):

> And it shall be that every living thing that moves, wherever the rivers go, will live..., and everything will live wherever the river goes.... Along the bank of the river, on this side and that, will grow all kinds of trees used for food; their leaves will not wither, and their fruit will not fail. They will bear fruit every month, because their water flows from the sanctuary. Their fruit will be for food, and their leaves for medicine. (Ezekiel 47:9, 12 NKJV)

The indwelling Holy Spirit is a river that is to flow from us, bringing life to everything He touches. There are probably countless ways to release God's presence into a situation, but I know of four main ones, the first of which we will review in today's devotion. However, let me say again that never are we put in a position where we control God. As I often remind people, He doesn't work for me—I work for Him. And let us never limit the ways in which God may work in our lives or in others' lives but be continually open to the Spirit's leading.

147

The first way to release the presence of God into a situation is through the spoken word. God's presence is released whenever we say what the Father is saying. That was the experience of Jesus and the example He gave us, which is also to be our experience and example. Once again, Jesus said, *"The words that I speak to you are spirit, and they are life"* (John 6:63). I also remind you of this statement from Psalm 107:20 (various translations): *"He sent His word and healed them."* The Healer is released into a situation by decree. We see this happen in the account of the centurion and his slave. That soldier's insight into authority, which he described to Jesus, was remarkable, especially for a Roman. His understanding gave a context for great faith, to which Jesus responded by saying his servant was healed. When the centurion arrived at home, he discovered his servant had been healed the moment Jesus said he was healed. (See, for example, Matthew 8:5–13.)

Perhaps you've been in a dire situation where you were gathered in a room with other family members or friends in fear and uncertainty. Then someone walked into that room and made one encouraging statement, and the atmosphere changed completely. This didn't happen only because the person shared a good idea. Concepts don't change atmospheres. But presence does. As the individual spoke, the presence of the Spirit of God was released into the room, and your outlook on the situation was transformed. A word spoken to bring encouragement sometimes carries the presence of God into a broken situation. Learning to yield to God's heart and mind is the only safe way to discover how to faithfully carry this God-given responsibility.

Overflow: God's presence is released whenever we say what the Father is saying.

Reading: Mark 10:46–52

Reflection: How might you change the way you approach the situations in your life if you kept this truth in mind: "Concepts don't change atmospheres. But presence does"?

_____

_____

_____

_____

_____

_____

_____

_____

_____

_____

_____

_____

_____

_____

_____

_____

_____

_____

DAY 47

RELEASING GOD'S PRESENCE, PART 2: TOUCH

"[Jesus] *stretched out His hand and touched* [the leper],
saying, 'I am willing; be cleansed.'
And immediately the leprosy left him."
—Luke 5:13 (NASB)

In yesterday's devotion, we saw that one way to release God's presence into a situation is through the spoken word. A second way is through touch. The Bible teaches us about the laying on of hands for various types of spiritual needs. It is sometimes the method God uses to ordain someone into ministry. For example, Moses imparted some of his authority onto Joshua. (See Numbers 27:17–22.) The literal word for the Hebrew term translated as *"authority"* in Numbers 27:20 is "majesty." Even more than that, it "refers to whatever or whoever is royally glorious."[10] Moses gave some of the majesty that God had placed upon him to Joshua so he could lead God's people in a supernatural way as Moses's successor.

In the New Testament, the apostle Paul and other church leaders ordained Timothy into service *"with the laying on of hands"* (1 Timothy 4:14 NKJV, NASB). Gifts were imparted to him that he was responsible to maintain. It became the assignment of the Lord for Timothy to keep these gifts active and in constant development.

---

10. *NKJV Spirit-Filled Life Bible*, 606.

The laying on of hands is also a practical way to impart a healing. Jesus said about those who believe in Him, *"They will lay hands on the sick, and they will recover"* (Mark 16:18 NKJV, NASB). Touching someone in Jesus's name is more than a symbolic act. Through the laying on of hands, we impart what we actually have to give: the presence of the Holy Spirit.

There are also biblical examples of Jesus being touched by someone who was seeking healing instead of His doing the touching Himself. This occurred not only with the woman who had the issue of blood but also with others who touched the hem of Jesus's garment. (See Matthew 14:34–36; Mark 6:56.) Additionally, people were healed or delivered after touching articles of clothing that the apostle Paul had worn. (See Acts 19:11–12.) Again, touching the clothing of Jesus or Paul was much more than a symbolic act. The Spirit of God will often saturate a cloth, similar to cloth being soaked in a natural river. The miracle anointing on a person's life can be received by a simple touch of the clothing in an act of faith. Each touch gives people access to a measure of presence that is in the cloth because it was touched by an anointed person.

Perhaps the most extreme example of this phenomenon is when the apostles laid hands on people who were then baptized in the Holy Spirit. (See, for example, Acts 8:14–17.) Such an encounter with God that forever marked their lives with the power of the Spirit was the result of a touch. Think of it: God's power and presence were released through the obedient touch of another human being. This testifies of the greatness of God, not the greatness of any individual. At the end of the day, all of these expressions are by the grace of God.

Overflow: Through the laying on of hands, we impart what we actually have to give: the presence of the Holy Spirit.

Readings: Luke 5:12–15; 7:11–17

Reflection: Where have you seen the presence of God manifest in anointing, healing, or in another way as the Holy Spirit worked through the means of human touch?

_____

_____

_____

_____

_____

_____

_____

_____

_____

_____

_____

_____

_____

_____

_____

_____

DAY 48

RELEASING GOD'S PRESENCE, PART 3: A PROPHETIC ACT

"When he showed [Elisha] the place, he cut off a stick and throw it in there, and made the iron float."
—2 Kings 6:6 (NASB)

Prophetic acts are found throughout Scripture, but they are often overlooked or considered incidental. *Prophetic act* is not a biblical term. It is simply a descriptor to help us identify something through which God flows. It is an act in the natural that releases something in the spiritual. And it is almost always unconnected logically to the intended outcome.

In 2 Kings, we find an example of a prophetic act in an incident involving Elisha:

> Now the sons of the prophets said to Elisha, "Behold now, the place before you where we are living is too limited for us. Please let us go to the Jordan and each of us take from there a beam, and let us make a place there for ourselves where we may live."… So he went with them; and when they came to the Jordan, they cut down trees. But as one was felling a beam, the axe head fell into the water; and he cried out and said, "Alas, my master! For it was borrowed." (2 Kings 6:1–2, 4–5 NASB)

Elisha had accompanied the other prophets as they cut down trees to build a dwelling where all of them could live. The head of the axe that one of the prophets was using fell off its handle and sank into the nearby Jordan River. *Lost.* This son of the prophets was particularly distressed by what happened because he had borrowed the axe. The desire in this illustration was the recovery of the axe head.

The prophet appealed to Elisha, who asked him where the axe head had fallen, then cut off a branch and threw it into the water, after which the lost axe head floated to the surface so it could be retrieved. (See verses 6–7.) You might throw branches into the water until Jesus returns and never again get a sunken axe head to float to the surface. Throwing the branch into the water didn't make the axe head swim. It was Elisha's following the leading of God's Spirit in a prophetic act that led to the miracle.

Another great example of a prophetic act is when the Israelites were fighting the Amalekites, who had attacked them in the wilderness. As long as Moses held his arms up in the air, Joshua and his army were winning the battle. But when Moses lowered his arms, they were losing. (See Exodus 17:8–13.) There is no logical connection between an army's victory and the raised hands of their leader. It does us no good to imagine that God will somehow act on our behalf because we're willing to do something unusual or unreasonable and say it's from Him. Obedience is the key on our end of the equation. We must listen to what God is telling us to do and then do it.

Overflow: A prophetic act is an act in the natural in obedience to God, unconnected to the outcome, that releases something in the spiritual.

Reading: Exodus 17:8–13

Reflection: Both Moses and Elisha engaged in prophetic acts that released supernatural victory and help. What kind of relationship with God must they have had in order to hear and obey Him in these instances?

_____

_____

_____

_____

_____

_____

_____

_____

_____

_____

_____

_____

_____

_____

_____

_____

_____

DAY 49

RELEASING GOD'S PRESENCE, PART 4: AN ACT OF FAITH

"And [Jesus] said to him, 'Go, wash in the pool of Siloam'
(which is translated, Sent). So he went and washed,
and came back seeing."
—John 9:7 (NKJV)

An act of faith is an action that illustrates our belief and trust in God. Unlike a prophetic act, it is directly connected to the desired outcome. When we were ministering in Weaverville, California, a man once came to the town theater where we held our meetings on Sundays. This man had fallen off his deck at home and seriously injured his ankle. He had crawled into his house and asked his wife to take him to the hospital because he was unable to put any weight on his leg without experiencing excruciating pain. The theater was on the way to the hospital, and the man knew we were meeting there that morning and wanted to see if God would heal him, so he asked his wife to stop there. Our service had just ended, so I was out front talking with people who were on their way home. The man's wife drove him to the curb where I was standing. He got out of the car, and, supporting himself on one leg, he held on to the passenger-side door of the car and explained the situation.

I prayed for him at least twice without seeing any progress at all. Then I had an impression that he needed to slowly put weight on the ankle as I prayed one more time. The idea of causing further injury to someone so they could prove their faith was a terrifying thought to me. But if the man did it slowly enough, he could monitor the situation on his own. He agreed. As I prayed again, he slowly put weight on his injured foot until he was able to stand on it without any pain. It was a great lesson for me as I saw that he had faith enough to come to the theater and to trust my suggestion. I actually saw the miracle happen as the coloring and shape of the ankle changed back to normal before my eyes.

The man wanted to be healed so he could walk without pain. Slowly placing weight on his foot was an act of faith that released the miracle. Jesus encouraged acts of faith with statements like *"Rise, take up your bed and walk"* (John 5:8 NKJV) and *"Go, wash in the pool of Siloam"* (John 9:7, various translations). Acts of faith release the hand of God in beautiful ways.

We need to caution people whenever they think their act of faith earns the miracle. People with this mindset often do foolish things trying to prove their faith, and it usually ends in disaster. I will only give someone a direction with risk when I sense it comes from the presence of God.

Each of the four actions we have reviewed—a spoken word, a touch, a prophetic act, and an act of faith—releases the power and presence of God into a situation. When He shows up, He works wonders, and His works are always redemptive in nature.

⌒

Overflow: Acts of faith release the hand of God in beautiful ways.

Reading: John 9:1–7

Reflection: What is the difference between an act of faith that is performed in obedience to God and a presumptuous act that is done merely to obtain a desired outcome? What are some ways you can tell the difference?

_____

_____

_____

_____

_____

_____

_____

_____

_____

_____

_____

_____

_____

_____

_____

_____

_____

DAY 50

THE FELT REALITY OF GOD'S ABIDING PRESENCE

"Your kingdom come.
Your will be done on earth as it is in heaven."
—Matthew 6:10 (NKJV)

Overflow is not only seen in ministry to others through spiritual gifts, acts of kindness, prayer, and so forth. One can always serve people by following the principles of God's Word and be somewhat effective in each of the areas I've mentioned. In other words, I can do these things and still be totally dry and far away from an *overflow lifestyle*. God honors His Word and our obedience, and good things happen. The overflow I'm talking about is more about the felt reality of His presence resting upon us. This affects and/or flows from our being, our presence. I realize that probably sounds strange to some, but consider this: people were healed by being exposed to Peter's shadow. (See Acts 5:15.) Why did this occur? There's no substance to a shadow, but the reality of the kingdom of God reveals this: our shadow will always release whatever overshadows us. Living in the reality of being filled with the Holy Spirit has an effect on our surroundings.

Many years ago, my office was across the street from an organic grocery store that was next to a post office. In the morning, I would walk from my office to the post office, often stopping by the store on my way back to buy items for lunch. I started pausing at the back door of the store to pray before entering. After becoming aware of God's presence upon me, I would enter the store and pick up the items I needed. This became a regular practice. One day, the owner, who had become a friend, called out to me while I was shopping, saying, "Bill, come over here." I walked over to where he was standing in the organic produce section, and he continued, "Whenever you walk into the store, something is different." I don't think I was more spiritual than other believers who shopped there. Nor do I think I was more filled with the Holy Spirit than the others. But I might have been the only one who intentionally waited until the Holy Spirit rested upon me before I entered. This so affected the atmosphere that the owner noticed. I explained to him that what he sensed was the presence of God.

In essence, this manifestation of the presence of God was a fulfillment of Jesus's promise in the all-important verse in the passage about the vines and the vinedresser: *"If you abide in Me, and My words abide in you, ask whatever you wish, and it will be done for you"* (John 15:7 NASB). As we learn to live in the felt realization of God's abiding presence and keep His Word at the forefront of our thoughts and meditations, we can ask for anything, and it will be done. The Holy Spirit equips us to have an influence on what happens in and through people, bringing about the fulfillment of the heart of the Father: *"On earth as it is in heaven"* (Matthew 6:10, various translations).

Overflow: Living in the reality of being filled with the Holy Spirit has an effect on our surroundings.

Reading: Acts 5:12–16

Reflection: Has anyone ever said they felt a change in the atmosphere when you were present in it? If so, in what way(s) (e.g., experiencing peace, calmness, clarity of thought, conviction of sin, or joy)?

_____

_____

_____

_____

_____

_____

_____

_____

_____

_____

_____

_____

_____

_____

_____

DAY 51

GOD'S UNMEASURABLE THOUGHTS TOWARD US

"How precious also are Your thoughts to me,
O God! How vast is the sum of them!"
—Psalm 139:17 (NASB)

The Holy Spirit comes to us from eternity with unlimited imagination, dreams, and plans. These aspects are beyond all human intelligence and brilliance, are motivated by a heart of love for us, and are measured by God's compassion and affection. Quite frankly, His thoughts and plans are beyond our capacity to fully experience, let alone comprehend. Again, to explore this vast universe called the mind of God will take all of eternity.

Such wonders are best explored through the heart. A surrendered heart easily receives and is never able to take the glory for itself. True worship is a place of deep surrender, a response to a God who is always good toward us. As a worshipper, King David experienced this deep spiritual well, setting a new "high-water mark" for human understanding of the heart of God. It only seems right that the man known for having a "heart after God" (see 1 Samuel 13:14) would be the one to clearly see God's heart for us, strikingly described in Psalm 139.

David discovered something about the reality of God's thoughts toward us that is impossible to fully grasp. But that is part of its beauty. It's the value of mystery, the unlimited expression that comes from a perfectly loving Father. We often stare up at the sky, looking at the stars, the Milky Way, the moon, meteors—all of it beheld in wonder, yet none of it completely comprehended. If I could fully understand any part of God's nature and purpose, He really wouldn't be all that noteworthy. Again, I would end up with a god who was about my size. Very unimpressive. On the other hand, through the Holy Spirit, we are invited to explore the inexhaustible resources of our Creator's love, ideas, and promises. David spoke of God's vast landscape of thoughts when he said:

> I will give thanks to You, for I am fearfully and wonderfully made; wonderful are Your works, and my soul knows it very well. My frame was not hidden from You, when I was made in secret, and skillfully wrought in the depths of the earth; Your eyes have seen my unformed substance; and in Your book were all written the days that were ordained for me.... How precious also are Your thoughts to me, O God! How vast is the sum of them! If I should count them, they would outnumber the sand. When I awake, I am still with You.   (Psalm 139:13–18 NASB)

God's thoughts are beyond grand, and their significance cannot be measured. His thoughts about us outnumber the grains of sand on all the seashores of the earth. Interestingly, our inner man is more conscious of God's thoughts and ways than we often realize. Accordingly, the psalmist confesses, *"My soul knows it very well."* Each person who is born again can anticipate the adventure of a lifetime, exploring the depths of God's mind for us for all eternity.

Overflow: The Holy Spirit comes to us from eternity with unlimited imagination, dreams, and plans.

Reading: Psalm 139:1–18

Reflection: What creative dreams and plans has God revealed to you? How do these dreams and plans reflect His heart of love?

_____

_____

_____

_____

_____

_____

_____

_____

_____

_____

_____

_____

_____

_____

_____

_____

_____

_____

DAY 52

A CREATIVE PARTNERSHIP

*"It has been given to you to know the mysteries of
the kingdom of heaven."*
—Matthew 13:11 (NKJV)

The Holy Spirit played a remarkable role in the creation of all things: *"In the beginning...the Spirit of God was hovering over the face of the waters"* (Genesis 1:1–2 NKJV). This imagery is likened to a mother hen who broods over her eggs. In doing so, she creates the ideal atmosphere for her chicks to hatch and thrive. Likewise, the Holy Spirit broods over many things in our lives, always producing the atmosphere necessary for a full expression of life-giving creativity. Being endowed with this creativity is a normal result of spending time in God's manifest presence.

This reality gives us brilliant insight into the nature and birthplace of creativity in the life of a believer. Being sons and daughters of the Creator affords us unique access to His gifts, callings, and anointings. We were made and redeemed for a creative partnership with the Father through His Spirit. Our creativity is directed through the God-given dreams and desires we have for our lives. Such dreams and desires are formed through countless influences, including our upbringing, relatives, friends, and experiences. All of these aspects are tools that, when guided and empowered by the Holy Spirit, can help to shape us into the creatives God always intended us to be.

Creativity tends to increase in the lives of those who find a problem to solve. It's not just about writing the next novel or painting a picture. While those types of artistic expressions are included, I am speaking more generally of the redemptive plan of God being worked into our lives so that we are moved by the condition of humanity and endeavor to solve its problems through innovation. New technologies, medical breakthroughs, inventions, and other solutions, as well as the kinds of things that add culture and beauty to our lives, all flow from a place of God-given creativity. And, according to the Scriptures, that place is best found in and through the presence of the Spirit of God.

Living in the felt realization of God's presence is the first step to entering into our inherent design, purpose, and promise. Thus, it is essential to learn to recognize His presence and live in the environment that is natural to all who abide in that presence. The second step is an intentional embracing of all that God says to us, whether through Scripture or directly by His inspiration. His abiding presence, along with the seed of the Word of God, which contains the full expression of His nature, work in us to bring about the fulfillment of the design and purpose that originated in God's heart for us.

Overflow: We were made and redeemed for a creative partnership with the Father through His Spirit.

Reading: Matthew 13:1–16

Reflection: What problems in your family, community, or the world has God laid on your heart to seek Him about so that you may help to solve them either directly or in a supportive role?

_____

_____

_____

_____

_____

_____

_____

_____

_____

_____

_____

_____

_____

_____

_____

_____

_____

DAY 53

HIS REDEMPTIVE TOUCH

"I have filled him with the Spirit of God, in wisdom, in understanding, in knowledge, and in all manner of workmanship."
—Exodus 31:3 (NKJV)

In the Old Testament, under the leadership of Moses, a tabernacle was built to serve the children of Israel as their "house of God" while they lived in the wilderness. God was very detailed in His design of the tabernacle, specifying the colors, fabrics, building materials, and quality of work the Israelites were to use. This tabernacle was to be unlike anything the Israelites had built previously because it was to house the presence of God Himself.

The work required for this building project was beyond natural human ability. Perhaps it could best be described in this way: human talent was necessary, but the supernatural influence on the human element was even more important. For me, this is the perfect description of the life of a believer in our times. We must offer to God all we are capable of doing, knowing that we need Him to add His immeasurable touch to everything we do.

In the story of the building of the tabernacle, enter a man named Bezalel. He is the first person the Bible mentions as being filled with the Holy Spirit of God. That is remarkable. I would have thought Moses or one of Israel's kings or prophets would have had that honor. Instead, it was an artist, a craftsman. God said of him:

And I have filled him with the Spirit of God, in wisdom, in understanding, in knowledge, and in all manner of workmanship, to design artistic works, to work in gold, in silver, in bronze, in cutting jewels for setting, in carving wood, and to work in all manner of workmanship.   (Exodus 31:3–5 NKJV)

This creative genius needed the Holy Spirit to be able to create at a level required for this assignment. And if that measure of anointing was available under an inferior covenant, then how much more should we expect God to give it to us under the better covenant established by the blood of Jesus?

When we are filled with the Spirit, we should experience an overall redemptive touch on our ability to love and serve the world around us well as we share creative solutions to the problems we face. Instead of desiring to be rescued out of the hell of this world's present chaos, perhaps we should stand more assertively in our place as creatives, knowing that God has provided solutions and invited us to pursue Him for them. This too is the work of the Holy Spirit.

Remember, Jesus said that it is the Father's good pleasure to give us the mysteries of the kingdom. (See Luke 12:32.) Perhaps this is the secret to John 15:7 (NKJV): *"If you abide in Me, and My words abide in you, you will ask what you desire, and it shall be done for you."* The outcome of this amazing promise is that we fulfill our role of being co-laborers with God Himself, who responds with answers to our prayers.

Overflow: We must offer to God all we are capable of doing, knowing that we need Him to add His immeasurable touch to everything we do.

Reading: Exodus 31:1–10

Reflection: What step of faith do you need to take, in obedience to God's leading, knowing that He will add His immeasurable touch to it in order to fulfill His purposes?

_____

_____

_____

_____

_____

_____

_____

_____

_____

_____

_____

_____

_____

_____

_____

_____

_____

_____

DAY 54

THE GIVER OF SPIRITUAL GIFTS

*"One and the same Spirit works all these things, distributing to
each one individually just as He wills."*
—1 Corinthians 12:11 (NASB)

As we read through the four Gospels, we see Jesus displaying
the works and wonders of a loving Father. His primary mission was
to reveal the Father. And the exercise of the gifts of the Holy Spirit
accomplishes this in a variety of ways.

In discussing the gifts of the Holy Spirit, I want to remind you
that, although Jesus is eternally God, in His earthly life, He chose to
restrict Himself to doing what He saw His Father doing and saying
what He heard His Father saying. In Acts 10:38 (NKJV, NASB),
Jesus is described as *"healing all who were oppressed by the devil, **for
God was with Him.**"* As we have discussed, this verse emphasizes
an all-important aspect of the gospel: Jesus became a man and set
an example that we could follow *if the same Holy Spirit is involved.*
Everywhere we see Jesus at work, we see the Holy Spirit at work.
Jesus's lifestyle was one of absolute dependency on the Father, and
it became the model for all who would follow Him.

If Jesus performed His miracles only as God, I am still impressed,
but I am only a spectator. When I realize that He performed them
as a man dependent on God, I am no longer satisfied to stay the way
I am. Even if I feel that I fall short in living this miracle lifestyle well,

I just don't have the right to change my assignment to something different or "easier" when Jesus's giving us this model to follow came at such an extreme cost.

The Holy Spirit is the One who took what Jesus was receiving from the Father (what the Father was saying and doing) and brought it into the practical by revealing the Father through Jesus's words and works. Jesus lived dependently upon the Father for everything He said and did. But it was the Holy Spirit, *the dove who remains* (see John 1:32–33), who made the miracle realm common through Jesus's daily life. And He wants to do the same through us.

The apostle Paul addressed this reality of the Holy Spirit working His gifts through us most clearly to the church at Corinth. The new believers there were accustomed to serving many gods. But through Paul's instruction, they were learning that all the various manifestations of the supernatural came from *the one Spirit*, not from a variety of spirits or gods.

In 1 Corinthians 12:6–11, Paul gave the believers a list of a number of gifts, or expressions, of the Holy Spirit. I don't believe this list was to limit the ways in which God works. But it does reveal His ways and His desire to work through every believer through supernatural means. My opinion is that because the Holy Spirit, the Giver of spiritual gifts, lives in every believer, it is possible for us to function in any of the gifts at any time. They are contained in His person, and He dwells with us.

⌒

Overflow: It was the Holy Spirit who made the miracle realm common through Jesus's daily life. And He wants to do the same through us.

Reading: 1 Corinthians 12:6–11

Reflection: Which gifts of the Holy Spirit have you functioned in? How did God use these gifts to help or build up others?

_____

_____

_____

_____

_____

_____

_____

_____

_____

_____

_____

_____

_____

_____

_____

_____

_____

_____

DAY 55

POWER IS THE PURPOSE

*"Behold, I am sending forth the promise of My Father
upon you; but you are to stay in the city until you are clothed
with power from on high."*
—Luke 24:49 (NASB)

My upbringing was Pentecostal/charismatic, and the traditional approach I was raised with is that speaking in tongues is the initial outward evidence of being baptized in the Holy Spirit. I see good reasons to believe that. I also see reasons not to be so dogmatic on the subject. I heard one of the fathers of the Pentecostal movement say that to emphasize speaking in tongues as the evidence of the baptism in the Spirit is equal to emphasizing getting wet in water baptism. It certainly happens as a byproduct of the experience. And it is a wonderful and necessary gift. But it's not the point. *Power* is. Being clothed with power was the reason behind the command to be filled with the Spirit. (See Luke 24:49; Acts 1:8.) This is why we are not only to be filled but also overflowing with the Spirit as channels of God's power in the world.

When we speak in tongues, the Holy Spirit prays through us in either a form of intercessory prayer or praise—such as when the disciples proclaimed *"the mighty deeds of God"* (Acts 2:11 NASB) at Pentecost. I'm certain that all of us have come to a place where we have prayed about an issue and have run out of words to fully express what's in our hearts regarding the matter. At those moments, we are painfully aware that there is more to say, but words fail us. Praying in tongues helps us at this point because the Holy Spirit prays through us with brilliant accuracy and power.

I'm also certain that all of us have come to a place where we can no longer fully express what is in our hearts for God Himself when we are offering Him praise. Worshipping in tongues takes us out of our place of lack (of insights, boldness, and faith) into an abundance that better represents God's nature. At such times, the Holy Spirit is the One who empowers and directs our worship, making it effective in ministering to God. And both expressions result in answers to prayer and deeper encounters with God through worship, leading to personal edification and strength.

If you have never been baptized in the Holy Spirit, let me encourage you: it is a free gift that enables each believer to represent Jesus more fully. It is not a badge of achievement or something that makes us superior to another. It is simply an immersion into the presence of God that makes boldness, endurance, and miracles a more normal expression of our faith. Because it is free, just ask. Ask Jesus to baptize you in the Holy Spirit. Take time in prayer and worship to honor Him for His promise. Receive it by faith, trusting in His goodness. And then put on your seat belt. You're in for the journey of a lifetime.

⌒

Overflow: Being clothed with power was the reason behind the command to be filled with the Spirit.

Reading: Acts 1:8

Reflection: Have you been baptized in the Holy Spirit, receiving the power that God desires to give you for living a victorious life and ministering to and for Him? If not, ask your heavenly Father for this baptism and receive it by faith. If you have already received the baptism, ask the Father for a fresh infilling of His Spirit today.

DAY 56

PRACTICAL HUMAN EXPERIENCE

"Pursue love, yet desire earnestly spiritual gifts."
—1 Corinthians 14:1 (NASB)

When we don't seem to exhibit spiritual gifts, part of the problem is that we tend to think these gifts will "come" to us. In other words, that some sort of sovereign act of God will force or drive us into the manifestation of a gift. Consider this: Chapter 12 of 1 Corinthians unveils brilliant teaching about the gifts. Chapter 14 expands on this teaching with more practical instruction. But sandwiched in between these two chapters is one of the most necessary chapters in the entire Bible: 1 Corinthians 13, the chapter on love. Why? Because the gifts are for the edification of the believer. Chapter 14 starts with, *"Pursue love, yet desire earnestly spiritual gifts"* (verse 1 NASB). This implies that gifts don't necessarily come to us automatically. They must be earnestly desired and sought after. And what greater motivation for pursuing these various manifestations of the Holy Spirit could there be than the motivation of love for the church—seeing each person edified and encouraged? The love chapter sets us up to pursue manifestations of the Holy Spirit for the right reason.

Thus, chapter 12 emphasizes that the gifts are given according to the will of the Holy Spirit. Chapter 14 emphasizes that they are given to those who earnestly desire and pursue them. That's not a contradiction. It's an expansion of a mysterious concept that is to help us better understand the partnership between the sovereignty of God and the desire and pursuit of His people. God's sovereignty reigns supreme. As God, He needs nothing from us. But He has written us into His plan, so our passions should mirror His will for us. Perhaps it should be said that we are able to pursue gifts because He first willed for us to live a lifestyle of exercising spiritual gifts, to His glory and the benefit of His people.

Being used by God is not about feeling better about ourselves or our spiritual maturity or significance or importance. The use of spiritual gifts illustrates a commitment to the people of God that says, "Love always seeks the best for others. And how could there be anything better than a supernatural display of God's heart for His people through ongoing manifestations of the Holy Spirit? Therefore, I will passionately pursue manifestations of the Spirit through my life."

It's important to realize that the revelation of the gifts in 1 Corinthians 12 didn't impart the gifts themselves. The list of gifts revealed what we can and must pursue. We often think we understand something because we can quote a principle about it that we've been taught. But a principle is not really understood until it is brought into practical human experience.

Overflow: What greater motivation for pursuing the various manifestations of the Holy Spirit could there be than the motivation of love for the church—seeing each person edified and encouraged?

Reading: Romans 12:3–9

Reflection: Are you ready to earnestly seek God and His spiritual gifts, asking Him to use you to minister to others in love? How will you begin to do so today?

_____

_____

_____

_____

_____

_____

_____

_____

_____

_____

_____

_____

_____

_____

_____

_____

_____

DAY 57

THE IMPORTANCE OF FAILURE

"Encourage the fainthearted, help the weak,
be patient with everyone."
—1 Thessalonians 5:14 (NASB)

I'm an Apple computer fan and have been for about thirty-five years. Like all major corporations of this nature, Apple Inc. has two basic parts of their company: (1) manufacturing and (2) research and development. The two branches of this corporation have two completely different sets of core values. For example, manufacturing has a core value of *zero defects*. They do not want four hundred thousand iPhones to be recalled because of flaws. But research and development's core value is that the developers are expected to fail. A lot. "Failure" in this sense would more accurately be described as *finding out what won't work*. If those doing the experiments don't fail, they can't possibly discover the full potential of their inventions or designs. The boundaries that make excellence possible are found on the edge of success, often made possible by discovering what doesn't work.

As believers, we have two basic parts to our lives as well, which we talked about earlier. These are the two legs we stand on: character and power. Both legs need to be of equal length, or we will limp. As sacrilegious as it sounds, we don't really want our character to be stronger than our power. And we certainly don't want our power to be greater than our character.

The realm of character is the manufacturing branch of the church, where we want zero defects. Again, it is the *Holy* Spirit who lives within us, so purity in our lifestyle—in our thoughts, ambitions, and behavior—must be pronounced. Ministry/power is the research and development branch of the church. To grow in serving the Lord and serving other people, especially in spiritual gifts, we are required to accept failure in the same way we expect a child to fall when they're learning to walk. After a ten-month-old takes two steps and falls, we cheer, pick them up, and encourage them to try again. Ministry really is a lot like that. And as long as we live in accountability and take responsibility for our actions, this approach will enable us to explore areas of life and ministry that we would never otherwise discover. It is religion—that spirit of perfectionism—that keeps so many believers from learning how to serve the Lord in realms of the supernatural. A fear of failure cripples too many people who live with the idea of *no failure* in ministry. They think that this is a sign of maturity, when in reality they have not failed because they have not tried.

I've just opposed perfectionism as a religious counterfeit to what God has called us to: excellence. But, in full disclosure, Jesus said, *"Therefore you are to be perfect, as your heavenly Father is perfect"* (Matthew 5:48 NASB). This wonderful command to *"be perfect,"* which is also an invitation by Jesus, can only be approached through the joy of loving and serving Him well. Responding to the inner workings of the Holy Spirit takes us toward perfection every single day of our lives.

Overflow: A spirit of perfectionism keeps so many believers from learning how to serve the Lord in realms of the supernatural.

Reading: Colossians 3:23–24

Reflection: Is perfectionism or a fear of failure keeping you from serving God and others through spiritual gifts? If so, after reading this devotion, what have you discovered about how God wants you to approach growing in the supernatural?

_____

_____

_____

_____

_____

_____

_____

_____

_____

_____

_____

_____

_____

_____

DAY 58

NO LONGER MUNDANE

"And we know that God causes all things to work together for
good to those who love God,
to those who are called according to His purpose."
—Romans 8:28 (NASB)

We live in two realities at all times: (1) the natural realm, which is the visible, tangible world in which we live—with its physical laws, principles, and boundaries—and (2) the supernatural realm, or the spiritual world, which is unseen but influences and affects all that we see and hear. While we exist within these two distinct realities, God exists in only one reality: the "supernaturally natural." It's all His. What is supernatural and unexplainable to us is perfectly natural and logical to Him. There is no distinction between the two. We have the opportunity to discover the joy of the supernaturally empowered natural elements of life. Nothing is mundane once God touches it!

I believe that one of our greatest journeys in life is to learn how to yield natural things to God's influence and find His delight in what normally would not seem to be the most exciting parts of our lives. We read in Proverbs, *"In all your ways acknowledge Him, and He will make your paths straight"* (Proverbs 3:6 NASB). *"In all your ways"*: in family relationships, positions of ministry and work, responsibilities, and hobbies—all of it. Recognize God as the source and inspiration in each of those things, and His hand will be released to influence and put a mark on your journey. If and when we involve Him in the simple and practical ways of life, they will receive His touch, and we will find greater meaning for every part of our lives.

God truly longs for us to live fully from a place of personal transformation, expressing the gifts and manifestations of the Holy Spirit to further edify and strengthen the people of God, to bring Him glory in all of life. This is our privileged assignment. The two elements of spiritual fruit and gifts give credibility to the gospel. The good news is for all. But it doesn't stop there. It doesn't stop with our becoming people of character or even people of supernatural gifting and power. God also wants to immerse us in His presence in such a way that everything about us is saturated with the God of wonders, the Holy Spirit who dwells in us and among us. Saturated with God on earth, who lives inside of every child of God. God's desire is to capture and repurpose our natural gifts, assignments, and functions.

Every experience and every relationship, good or bad, every past success as well as every failure, goes into the recipe of the Master Chef, who makes *"all things work together for good"* (Romans 8:28 NKJV, KJV). Many of these ingredients have a bitter taste in themselves. But when God redeems them, He repurposes them until they become the gold standard of what He can make out of our lives. This is especially true of our natural gifts. They become repurposed until they give Him place to be revealed in the simplest and most practical ways.

⌁

Overflow: We have the opportunity to discover the joy of the supernaturally empowered natural elements of life.

Reading: Proverbs 3:5–6

Reflection: Have you yielded any natural things to God's influence and then seen Him manifest His power and grace in them? If so, what were they, and how did God receive glory through them?

_____

_____

_____

_____

_____

_____

_____

_____

_____

_____

_____

_____

_____

_____

_____

_____

_____

_____

_____

DAY 59

A TREE OF LIFE

"Desire fulfilled is a tree of life."
—Proverbs 13:12 (NASB)

The Holy Spirit helps us to align our desires with God's and realize our dreams. He continuously works to conform us into the image of Jesus so we can be shaped and qualified to carry out those dreams.

We often pray great prayers. Big prayers. My conviction is that when we do so, the Holy Spirit immediately begins to work on us, making us into someone who can survive and thrive under the weightiness of the answer. The glory of God upon a person either exposes cracks in that person's foundation (for the purpose of mending them) or establishes the individual in a way that they are absolutely committed to having God receive all the glory.

All of this seems to be connected to this familiar verse from Proverbs 13:12 (NASB): *"Hope deferred makes the heart sick, but desire fulfilled is a tree of life."* Solomon wrote that having fulfilled desires connects us to a *"tree of life."* And Jesus said that fulfilled desires give us fullness of joy. (See John 16:24.) These are two sides of the same coin because we were designed to have desires and then to see those desires fulfilled by a loving Father, reinforcing our identity in Him and giving us abundant life, measured by joy.

Because we were designed for such a heavenly partnership, it is affirming whenever we see our God-birthed desires answered and fulfilled. It is the Holy Spirit who helps us discern whether our desires are born of God or whether we are trying to use Scripture to persuade Him to let us have our own way. We all need the help of the Holy Spirit during this journey because the full effect of God's purpose for our lives will have such a significant impact on us and the world around us. This area of fulfilled desire is a major threat to the enemy's influence on the earth and is therefore a chief target of his. In the answers to our prayers, our heavenly Father is revealed as a loving Father. We owe that revelation of God to the world, so we must pray to receive answers for ourselves and others.

Fulfilled desires have another benefit that I've only recently recognized: they add days to our lives and strength to our days. *"Who satisfies your years with good things, so that your youth is renewed like the eagle"* (Psalm 103:5 NASB). There's something medicinal about fulfilled desires and dreams—answers to prayer. Our realization that we have received God's favor, along with our increased sense of identity and purpose, serves to bring more strength and even years to our lives. We've all seen those who die soon after losing their reason for living. The opposite is also true: strength and increase of days come to those who delight in the benefit of fulfilled God-dreams. The great joy of being used by God is surpassed only by His manifest presence itself.

Overflow: We were designed to have desires and then to see those desires fulfilled by a loving Father.

Reading: Psalm 103:1–5

Reflection: Have you experienced God changing you before answering your prayers? If so, in what specific ways did He shape you and prepare you for the answers?

_____

_____

_____

_____

_____

_____

_____

_____

_____

_____

_____

_____

_____

_____

_____

_____

_____

DAY 60

DOING THE WORKS OF OUR FATHER

"The works that I do in My Father's name,
they bear witness of Me."
—John 10:25 (NKJV)

Let us keep in mind that every time we see Jesus performing a miracle in the New Testament, we are witnessing the Trinity at work. Jesus only did what He saw the Father doing. That means it was the Father who revealed what, how, and when a miracle should be done. Not only that, but we are also witnessing the work of the Holy Spirit, who was the *dunamis* (power) from heaven resting upon Jesus and flowing through Him that made the miracle possible. And the works testified to who Jesus was:

> *If I do not do the works of My Father, do not believe Me; but if I do, though you do not believe Me, believe the works, that you may know and believe that the Father is in Me, and I in Him.* (John 10:37–38 NKJV)

This was a powerful statement. Jesus, inspired by the Holy Spirit, announced to all those who were in the crowd gathered to hear Him that if He didn't do the works of the Father, they weren't required to believe in Him. A thorough study of the gospel of John will show that when the writer speaks of the works of the Father, he is without question speaking of the miracle realm. Consider this: The prophets

189

foretold of Jesus's coming, creation testified of His coming, the intercessors spoke of His coming, and the angels declared His coming. There are probably more who testified about Him that I missed. And yet Jesus announced that the crowd didn't have to believe any of the credible witnesses that the Father had sent and had used throughout history if this one additional element was not in place: miracles. So Jesus said, in effect, "If the miracles aren't there, you don't have to believe."

*God anointed Jesus of Nazareth with **the Holy Spirit** and with power, who went about doing good and healing all who were oppressed by the devil, **for God was with Him**.*

(Acts 10:38 NKJV)

Miracles were the evidence that the Spirit of God was with Jesus, and they are the evidence that He is with us. I look forward to the day when the church—which has now come to know the same Father that our Elder Brother Jesus does, and which is empowered by the same Holy Spirit that Jesus was—would have the courage to declare to this world, "If we do not do the works of our Father, you do not have to believe our message."

As we travel this journey, the Holy Spirit helps us in our weaknesses. That is as good a job description of the Holy Spirit as we'll ever hear, as there is nothing I have been called to do in which I am not weak. He who is power, who is holiness, is longing to manifest more fully through each of us so that Jesus might be seen for who He really is. In all the earth.

⌒

Overflow: Miracles were the evidence that the Spirit of God was with Jesus, and they are the evidence that He is with us.

Reading: John 10:22–42

Reflection: What evidence of the supernatural or miraculous does your life reflect so that others will believe in the reality of Jesus and His message? How can you rely more fully on the Holy Spirit to manifest the life of Jesus through you?

ABOUT THE AUTHOR

Bill Johnson is the Senior Leader of Bethel Church in Redding, California, where he has ministered since 1996, and the cofounder of the Bethel School of Supernatural Ministry (BSSM). A fifth-generation pastor, Bill serves a growing number of churches that have partnered for revival. This apostolic network has crossed denominational lines in building relationships that enable church leaders to walk in both purity and power. Bill is also the popular author of numerous books, including *The Holy Spirit*, *When Heaven Invades Earth*, and *Hosting the Presence*. His priority in life has been to learn how to host the presence of God and minister to Him. He is passionate about seeing the kingdom of heaven invade earth across all spheres of influence, with the wisdom of God displayed through the church, government, education, and the arts. Bill travels extensively to share what he has learned through his experience, with the conviction that the only way to increase what has been given is to give it away.